# The Austin Haley Story

# The Austin Haley Story

## A Family Confronting Unthinkable Tragedy

**Renee and Jack Haley**

TATE PUBLISHING & *Enterprises*

*The Austin Haley Story*
Copyright © 2010 by Renee and Jack Haley All rights reserved.

No part of this publication may be reproduced, stored in a retrieval system or transmitted in any way by any means, electronic, mechanical, photocopy, recording or otherwise without the prior permission of the author except as provided by USA copyright law.

All scripture quotations, unless otherwise indicated, are taken from the New King James Version®. Copyright © 1982 by Thomas Nelson, Inc. Used by permission. All rights reserved.

The opinions expressed by the author are not necessarily those of Tate Publishing, LLC.

Published by Tate Publishing & Enterprises, LLC
127 E. Trade Center Terrace | Mustang, Oklahoma 73064 USA
1.888.361.9473 | www.tatepublishing.com

Tate Publishing is committed to excellence in the publishing industry. The company reflects the philosophy established by the founders, based on Psalm 68:11, *"The Lord gave the word and great was the company of those who published it."*

Book design copyright © 2010 by Tate Publishing, LLC. All rights reserved.
*Cover design by Blake Brasor*
*Interior design by Blake Brasor*

Published in the United States of America
ISBN: 978-1-61566-992-9
1. Self help, Death, Grief, Bereavement
2. Biography & Autobiography, Personal Memoirs
10.2.23

# Dedication

This book is lovingly dedicated to all our children and future grandchildren in memory of Austin.

Remember to always keep God first in your lives, and He will bless you in ways you have never even imagined.

Also, we dedicate this book to any person who may be going through an unthinkable situation in his or her own life.

# Acknowledgments

To all the staff at Tate Publishing: Thank you for seeing the potential of this book.

To my wonderful father, Jack Tracy: We appreciate you being an outstanding informational contributor to this book and a wonderful grandpa to our children.

To my mother, Cheryl Tracy, and my mother-in-law, Bettie Haley: Thank you for the many hours and days of editing the manuscript and being outstanding grandmothers to our children.

To each and every one of our family and friends: We appreciate you lifting us up and giving us strength each and every day through hugs, gifts, flowers, food, cards, or simply using your talents in various ways, including editing skills, to encourage and comfort us.

To the countless hundreds of thousands worldwide, including all of those in our own community, who have prayed for us: We want you to know how your support gave us strength and your prayers gave us peace. We literally felt your prayers. We could not have made it without you.

To Noble Assembly of God in our hometown of Noble, Oklahoma: We thank you for ministering and reaching out to our family. You are a wonderful home-church family. We love you all.

To the pastors of Noble Assembly of God: We want to give you a special thank you for your prayers and also for teaching Austin about God, Jesus, and the Holy Spirit.

To the other churches in and around our community: You uplifted us so much with your thoughts, prayers, and many ways of showing us your love.

To all of Austin's dear friends: He loved you all so much. Thank you for playing with and loving him the way you did. Love the Lord with all your heart, mind, and soul; you will be reunited with him someday.

To Barbara Allen, Austin's aunt: We appreciate you using your talent as a barber who had cut Austin's hair his entire life and trimmed his hair at the funeral home after his death. It made him look handsome and peaceful. It meant so much to us being able to keep hair from his first haircut and also his last.

To Noble Public Schools, with a special thanks to Katherine I Daily Elementary School, Austin's teacher, Ms. Brown, and her assistant, Ms. Hart: We appreciate the many hours you spent loving Austin and teaching him in Pre-K.

To Amy Tennison: Thank you so much for the T-Shirts with Austin's name and his #23 you designed and sold in memory of our son.

To Lorenz Photography in Noble: Thank you for taking the time to produce our book cover photos.

# Table of Contents

Foreword .............................................. 11
Prologue .............................................. 15
Confronted with the Unthinkable Tragedy ................ 21
Comfort your Grieving Children ......................... 39
Forgive ............................................... 53
Keep the Faith ........................................ 59
Allow Yourself Time to Grieve .......................... 65
Recognize Bad Things Also Happen to Good People ........ 75
Give and Receive ...................................... 89
Focus on the Good Things .............................. 99
Provide Strength and Comfort to the Grieving ........... 111
Where are we Now? (Concluding Thoughts) ................ 117
When Adversity Comes Against You
    and the Keys to Overcome It ...................... 125
A Father's Memories ................................... 139
Grandparent's Thoughts and Memories of Austin .......... 145
Appendix: Comforting Bible Verses
    during Grief and Sadness ......................... 153
Unforgettable Quotes from Family and Friends ........... 161
Endnotes .............................................. 163

# Foreword

What you are about to read is a story that I wish had never happened; a senseless tragedy that reminds us that life is unfair at times, regardless of who you are or what you believe. Yet it is precisely this unfairness that demands that we put our trust in the Lord Jesus Christ. Like a sparkling gem against a black-velvet background is the faith of the Haley family in the midst of the blackest of circumstances.

I had the privilege of being at the hospital shortly after Austin was born in October of 2001 and dedicating him to the Lord a few weeks later. Each Sunday I got to see him and his family faithfully worshiping the Lord in the worship services and Austin quoting a Bible verse from the platform with the microphone on Sunday evenings. During the week, I would see Austin at Kidz Konnection, our church childcare center, playing and learning and growing up. On Friday, August 3, I had driven the older children from Kidz Konnection on the church bus to the park. I remember Austin was the last one off the bus when we returned, and I asked him if he had a good time. He said he did, but he seemed a little sad, which was unlike him. I talked with him a little and said good-bye, and he went inside. I never dreamed that good-bye would be my last one, for only a few hours later I was at the hospital beside his grieving family, trying to make some sense out of it all.

What you will read in this inspiring book is the story behind the story. You will cry and you will smile and you will be amazed as you read these pages. Inside Austin Haley was a deep faith that affected his life and the lives of those around him every day. This faith in the Lord Jesus Christ is also what has carried his wonderful and loving parents, Jack and Renee, and his great little brother, Dalton, through these times. The grandparents, aunts and uncles, and cousins all will say the same thing: without the Lord and his amazing grace and miracle-working power, they would not be able to endure.

I trust that you will be blessed as you read this book and understand that "blessed is the man who trusts in the Lord, whose confidence is in Him," (Jeremiah 17:7).

—Pastor Steve Lance, Noble Assembly of God Church

# Prologue

Written February 2001, six months prior to Austin's birth:
I prayed for God to keep Austin and protect him even before he was born.

## How Very Often I Have Dreamed of You

How very often I have dreamed of you,
To hold you in my arms,
To kiss you on your cheek,
And to comfort all day long.

How very often I have dreamed of you,
A world of perfect bliss,
To hold your tiny hand in mine
And give a little kiss.

How very often I have dreamed of you
My little boy or girl
With silky black hair like Daddy's
Or like Mama's with reddish curls.

How very often I have dreamed of you.
Please, God, keep my baby safe.

I can't wait to hold you in my arms
And gaze into your face.

Renee Haley

Dear Austin,

You were a light to your family and to so many people who knew you—even to thousands of people in the world who didn't know you. Your five years of life have made such a dynamic impact on lives everywhere. As we reflect on your short life of five years, nine months, and ten days, you have made us so proud. We were amazed to see how you matured in the Lord at a very young age. As parents, we loved you and taught you to love Jesus. At the same time, you were teaching *us* that being parents of a little boy like you, Austin, was the greatest gift that we could ever obtain in life—definitely a gift from God. We experienced love for you beyond what any words could ever express; in turn, you loved us back. Times we spent laughing and playing will always be remembered. What a blessing we will share, our little man, when we can hold you in our arms in heaven—together forever. We will meet you at heaven's open gates. What a day that will be!

We love you so much,
Mama and Daddy

# Prologue

"What!"

My father repeats a second time: "Honey, someone shot Austin right in the head. I don't think he's going to make it."

"*No!*" I take off running as quickly as I can toward the pond where I had thought Austin was, not taking a moment of breath from the scream.

My father abruptly stops me with fear in his voice, saying, "No, don't go down there! The shooter may still be there!" I'm torn in two. Should I continue running toward the pond where I'm thinking my son is, or should I not because someone may shoot me? As a mother, I knew I had to render help to my son, even if there was danger involved for me.

Just then I hear my father say, "I've got Austin here in the back of the Polaris." Trembling as though an earthquake is taking over my body…everything is happening in slow motion. At any moment I'm going to break—there's no doubt about it. My husband hears my screams; he runs toward me.

> Out of breath, I barely am able to speak. "Someone shot Austin while he was at the pond!"

Putting a hand on each of my shoulders, he asks, "What? What happened?"

Out of breath, I barely am able to speak. "Someone shot Austin while he was at the pond!"

We both run back toward our house, where Austin is lying in the back of my father's dark-green Polaris all-terrain vehicle. I watch as my husband collapses to his knees on the ground near Austin. Our two-year-old son, Dalton, places his hands over his ears, screaming, "No, no! Not my bubba!" My father shakes his head as he lifts up his bloodstained hands, trying to make sense of it all and saying, "I am going to kill the person who did this to my grandson!" Grandpa Jim is still searching for the murderer through the trees. I rush inside of the house to call 911, bringing Dalton with me to keep him protected from the gunman located outside. I then run back outside, where I see my son, Austin, once again. I look for movement. Every once in a while it seems I see his chest moving. I can't tell if it really is or if it is my overwhelmed mind just hoping it is. His eyes are half open, almost as if he is looking at me for comfort and help. Is Austin really not going to make it, or is he in tremendous pain, unable to say a word? I am unsure, but I know where to turn. I place my hands on Austin's bloodstained chest, and looking straight up to heaven, I pray, "Oh, God, as his mama, I am unable to help him. God, you can do anything! Please, take away all of his pain. Please, God, help him!" My overwhelmed mind seems to give way, immediately flashing back to a series of thoughts from before...

...October 24, 2001, at 12:09 in the afternoon I gave birth to a seven-pound-two-ounce bouncing baby boy with brown hair and chocolate-brown eyes. I was finally a mama of the most adorable baby I had ever seen in my life. Minutes after his birth, our family all entered the room. We gathered in a circle and began his life of serving Jesus by praying and singing this song: *"Jesus loves me, this I know. For the Bible tells me so. Little ones to him belong. They are weak, but He is strong. Yes, Jesus loves me. Yes, Jesus loves me. Yes, Jesus loves me. The Bible tells me so."*

With his tiny eyes wide open and peering around the room, he seemingly already knew the name of Jesus.

As he continued his life of a precious baby, a busy toddler, and a young boy, I began calling him "my little man." He became so grown up for his age. Sometimes I would think he was teaching me instead, especially when it came to knowing how to live life serving God. He would quote a different Bible verse in church every Sunday night. Austin would climb the steps to the platform, speaking loudly and clearly in the microphone, "My name is Austin Haley, and my Bible verse is…" His favorite was Jeremiah 17:7: "Blessed is the man who trusts in the Lord, whose confidence is in him." As a reward for quoting the verse, I watched as he rummaged through the candy, often looking for a bag of Skittles, his favorite.

Out on the Pre-K playground, he would climb to the highest part of the big toy and wait for a crowd to gather. At that time, he would ask his young congregation, "Does everybody here know Jesus?"

A shy child peered around the corner and said, "No, I don't know Jesus."

"You need to ask Him in your heart. He's the best superhero of them all!" Austin assured the boy.

Austin held his new baby brother, Dalton, in the hospital for the first time on September 22, 2004, on the day of Dalton's birth. They exchanged gifts. Austin gave Dalton a little toy hammer that he had chosen for him. Dalton, in return, gave Austin a doctor's kit that he just *knew* Dalton picked out himself. At that moment they became the best of friends—inseparable from then on. Austin began referring to Dalton as "little brother," and when Dalton got old enough, he always called Austin "Bubba." They did everything together—played with puzzles, played on the swing set, ate together, watched TV—I mean everything! One year, Austin chose to be Batman for Halloween, and Dalton decided he wanted to be Robin. Austin always held Dalton's hand and spoke to him with such a soft, sweet voice. Dalton adored Austin, everything about him.

Just after Austin's fifth birthday, he came home from daycare and was hungry, so he was searching for a snack in the pantry. I was heading down the hallway when he had thought I called his name. He peered around the door of the pantry and said, "Yes, Mama?"

I told Austin, "Baby, Mama didn't call you."

He said, "Oh, okay" and began to look in the pantry again for something to eat. After one more minute, he looked at me again, and he said, "Mama, you keep calling my name. Do you want something?" I realized then that he was having an encounter very similar to Samuel in the Bible.

I told him, "Son, *I* was not calling your name, but I do know who is. It is God. You need to answer him and tell him you are listening." He was amazed as Jack and I told him about the story of Samuel, and he later told me that evening he *did* know it was really God calling him.

The first day of this summer, I sat down with Austin and asked him for a wish list of the things he would like to do before kindergarten began. He gave me a list of about thirty things, including going fishing with Grandpa, taking Dalton to Perfect Swing (he always wanted to please his brother before himself), shopping with his grandma, aunt, and cousins, and spending time with his nanny and best friends. His list was so simple and loving toward the people he cherished. We had just finished that list.

Two weeks before Austin was taken from us, he began asking some very detailed questions of heaven, such as, "Mama, how do we get from here to heaven?"

I told him, "It happens as fast as that." I snapped my fingers. "Some people actually see a very bright light just before they pass away." I could tell through his eyes that he was thinking about this very intensely, and he got quiet for a long period of time. Later that same day, he was talking about his favorite colors. He loved coloring everything black and gray. He let me know why he loved those colors by saying, "Mama, if you will look around, almost everything has the color black or gray on it somewhere."

I glanced around the room at various objects and replied, "You know, Son, you are right. I've never really thought about it, but almost everything *does* include the colors black or gray." Austin was pleased with my response—smiling gently. I noticed the smile somewhat faded as he continued, "Will the colors black and gray be in heaven?" I told him I was sure they would be, and he continued naming off other colors to see if they were there also. I assured him that heaven was filled with an array of colors, and I believed we would see every one of them. That evening as I was putting him into his bed, I handed him his soft bear blanket that he loved to move between his thumb and his first two fingers as he went to sleep. He asked me again another question about heaven: "Mama, can I take my blanket to heaven?"

I told him, "You can have as many blankets in heaven as you would like." He told me that he wanted his, and I let him know I was sure God could make that happen. He smiled, said his prayer, and looked so comfortable underneath his bear blanket that Grandma and Mamaw bought him when he was born.

One week later, I took Austin into Mardell, a Christian bookstore, and the first thing he wanted to do was look at the Bibles. Austin loved Bibles. He carried his Bible—sometimes more than one Bible—with him everywhere, even to the shopping mall. I continued showing Austin one with pictures, and for some reason, he did not show any interest in Bibles with pictures. While holding the camouflaged Bible at the end of our ten-minute discussion, he said, "Mama, I don't care about the pictures. I just want to know what the words say." His words touched my heart, so before I knew it, I was purchasing the Bible. On the way home he clutched his new possession tightly in his arms and made the statement about the camouflaged cover: "Now I'm in the Lord's Army." We came home with that Bible, and he loved it more than any toy, staring at the map on the back page for hours at a time.

Two days before the gunshots echoed through my ears, Austin and I were both sitting in the living room, he in my recliner and I on the floor. I overheard him saying the most precious prayer, earnestly repeating over and over again, "I love you, God. I love you, Jesus…"

I looked at him with tears in my eyes, and I said, "Austin, that was such a beautiful prayer. God and Jesus love to hear you talk to them like that."

He got slightly embarrassed, and he told me he didn't know I could hear him. A couple minutes later, he said, "Mama, I have a question. I have Jesus in my heart and I have God in my heart, but when am I going to have the Holy Spirit in my heart?"

I told him, "That prayer was directly from your heart, Son. Continue praying just like that. God, Jesus, and the Holy Spirit hear your prayers."

..."Ma'am? Ma'am? We are going to need to take your son to the hospital immediately. We are meeting MetaFlight at the high school football field about a block away. We have to hurry. A gunshot wound to the head is not good. He has lost a tremendous amount of blood. We'll meet you at the hospital as quickly as possible!"

# Confronted with the Unthinkable Tragedy

On August 3, 2007, our day began very unusually. I am a sixth-grade English teacher, and on this day the principal had scheduled a meeting with the faculty to discuss our curriculum for the upcoming school year. I took our children to our church daycare, so I could attend the meeting. Since Austin and Dalton were used to attending the childcare center, they normally would be excited to see their friends once again. But this day was different from the very beginning.

As I awoke Austin, I was expecting him to lay his head in my lap, look up at me with his large chocolate brown eyes, and say his usual, "I love you so much, Mama." He did this almost every morning in his tired little voice. But that did not happen. Instead, he said, "Mama, this is going to be a very bad day." Tears began to stream down his face, and I began getting concerned. This was not the usual response I would get from Austin about attending daycare for the day. Normally, I would take the boys to eat breakfast at Kidz Konnection Daycare, but since he was so upset, I decided it would be much better for Austin to eat breakfast at home. Tears continued streaming down my little boy's face, dripping into his cereal bowl.

> Instead, he said, "Mama, this is going to be a very bad day."

I was perplexed because I had never seen him this upset before. I asked him to sit in my lap, and I rocked him, holding him tightly while continuing my questions:

"Son, what is wrong?"

"I don't know," he said through his sobbing.

"Do your friends treat you right at daycare?"

"Yes."

"You like your teachers, don't you?"

"Yes."

"So, you *do* like the daycare and playing with your friends?"

"Yes."

"So what is wrong, baby? Please tell Mama."

I began to cry along with Austin because I knew he was upset about *something*.

"I don't know. I am just going to miss you, Daddy, and Dalton *so* much."

I cuddled him closely while rocking him for another five minutes or so before he decided to crawl down to the living room floor and finish his cereal; it was difficult for him to finish eating because he continued to cry as he ate. He had large tears dripping from his face and splashing into his cereal bowl. After he finished eating, I took him and Dalton to the daycare, only three minutes away from our house in Noble, Oklahoma. As I was checking them in for the day, I looked down, and he began to cry again. I did not understand; this was extremely unusual. Normally, he would run in (he would always run; he never walked anywhere) and begin to talk and play with each one of his friends. I lifted him up into my arms as we both began to weep. I almost decided not to attend the meeting at the school. Again, I asked the same question: "Son, what is wrong?"

He repeated, "I don't know, but, Mama, I am going to miss you, Daddy, and Dalton *so* much."

I thought he was upset because it was going to be late in the afternoon before I would be able to pick him up. I reassured him that it would not be too long before I was able to come and take him home since it was only a short meeting. He looked at Kim, who was working the front desk at the time. She would always greet Austin and Dalton with a loving smile and hug as they walked through the door to the daycare. She was now crying because she noticed how upset we both were. I said, "Kim, I don't know what is wrong. He has been upset all morning."

Austin asked Kim, "Can I play with Dalton today?" Normally, my two boys would be in different rooms due to their age discrepancy, but she said, "Of course! We will find a way to make that happen." Austin finally had a little smile as he heard this.

I tried consoling him even more by asking him, "Austin, what do you want to do when we get home? I will do anything you want." He had two wishes: "I want you to push me on the swing behind our house, and I want to go to the pond." I let him know we would make that happen. He was much happier knowing we would spend time together later that evening, so I gave Austin and Dalton a kiss goodbye and left to attend the meeting at Curtis Inge Middle School, about two minutes away from the daycare in Noble.

About 4:00 p.m. I was so excited to pick up the boys at the daycare. I knelt down to give them a really big hug as they ran into my open arms, almost knocking me over. We all began to laugh. Austin and Dalton were always so excited to see Jack or me at the end of the day. Normally, Jack would pick them up, but since I left the school early, I went by and got the boys. Kim was allowing Austin to pick out a piece of candy from the "candy store" located at the daycare, and he asked, "Is it okay if I get Dalton some candy too?" Normally, the candy store would only be available to the school-age children. He was always so caring for everybody, especially when it came to his two-year-old brother, Dalton. She said, "Well, of course you can." He was so excited to see Dalton's smile after receiving the candy.

As soon as we got home, Austin sweetly stated, "I am going to give everyone in my family a hug and a kiss." As he climbed the stairs to see Daddy in the computer room, Austin opened the upstairs door and took a long look at his daddy. Later, Jack described it as a look of complete sadness that swept across his face. Jack was trying to understand if something bad had just happened. After Austin looked at him a few seconds, he said, "I love you, Daddy" and gave him a hug and a kiss, just like he said he was going to do. Jack replied, "I love you too, baby." Not long after, our family left to eat at a Souper Salad restaurant, where we all had a great Friday-night meal together. Austin reminded me of the promises I made earlier that morning about pushing him on the swing and feeding the fish at the pond. I reassured him that I had not forgotten.

We returned home at approximately 6:45 p.m. The boys and I went into the two-acre property in the backyard where our swing set was located, and my husband decided to go out and work in his shop for a little while, where he was working on his hobby of restoring classic cars. As I had promised, I pushed Austin and Dalton on the swing as long as they wanted while practicing Austin's counting to one hundred. We also played in the sandbox, making some castles and using shovels to design rivers and mountains in the wet sand. As we were digging, I began hearing voices at the neighbors' house. I did not think much about it since the housing addition was located directly behind our house, where we can usually see children playing in their backyard. I continued hearing a muffled conversation approximately three houses to the south. I heard broken statements behind a small line of trees: something about a snake … a hole … ask for help. I whispered to Austin and Dalton, "Shh, I think somebody may need help with a snake or something. Be quiet for just a minute." At that moment, I heard nothing more. The kids were getting tired of playing outside at this point, so we decided to go back inside the house.

I turned on our television in the living room to watch one of Austin's favorite shows, *SpongeBob Square Pants*. Austin was in my recliner drinking juice for approximately two minutes while Dalton was trying to figure out how to put the puzzle together that Austin had begun a couple hours before. Usually my husband mows, but I had decided to mow the front lawn to get a little exercise. Not long after I started mowing, I saw my dad and grandpa approaching our house on my father's Polaris Ranger (i.e., a small ATV). This could mean only one thing: he was going to ask the boys if they wanted to go to the family-owned pond approximately two hundred yards away from our home. My parents live nearby, so this was a usual event that took place at least twice a week. I quickly turned off the mower and rushed inside to give our boys the good news. "Austin and Dalton, guess what? Grandpa and Grandpa Jim are here if you want to go to the pond!" Austin quickly jumped out of the recliner, smiling from ear to ear, and eagerly said, "Mama, this was my last wish! Come on, Dalton. Let's go!" As I helped both of my sons climb on to the ATV, I asked Austin if he had his shoes on because they were ready so quickly. He reassured me that he did by pointing to the shiny orange and black shoes.

My dad asked me, "Honey, would you like to go down to the pond with us?" Normally I would, but on that day I decided to stay behind and get a little more mowing done in the front yard before it got too dark to see, as dusk was fast approaching. All was peaceful, although I could still hear muffled voices behind me at the neighbors' house. Since the pond was nearby, I could also hear my children giggling as the fish splashed around the dock in search of fish food being thrown in the water. I was humming to a Christian song my husband had playing in his shop near the house as I made my fourth circle around the lawn with the lawn mower. My boys were at the pond nearly five minutes when I heard someone yell, "Fire in the hole!" Earlier, I had heard them speaking of a snake and a hole. *Is something on fire?* I questioned myself silently in my mind. I was trying to make sense of it all, when suddenly I heard a gunshot that rattled my entire body and vibrated me from my head to my toes. It was just after 7:40 p.m. on Friday, August 3, 2007.

"Oh no," I said aloud to myself. "I hope nobody just committed suicide." I continued pushing the lawnmower as I began praying for whoever had just shot the gun. "Lord, please let them be okay." I very briefly thought of my family at the pond and listened for any unusual noises, but I thought I heard my dad say something such as, "We are okay down here," so I thought everything was fine. (Later I realized he said something different.) The gunshot sounded as if it was near our house. Approximately six seconds after the gunshot, I heard a second gunshot. It startled me again, and I felt uneasy, but I told myself the person with the gun was most likely target shooting. However, I knew they should not be shooting a gun inside of city limits directly in the middle of a residential area where we were living. I was making the fifth round with the push lawnmower when my Dad rapidly drove up to me in the ATV with beet-red eyes and yelled the echoing words I so wanted to be untrue: "Honey, someone shot Austin right in the head, and I don't think he's going to make it."

"*No!*" I took off running toward the pond where I thought Austin was. My body was trembling like an earthquake. At any moment I was going to break; there was no doubt about it. I had to let my husband know. Jack heard my scream and came running toward me, asking, "What? What happened?" We both turned around, running toward Austin as I gave him the horrifying news: "Someone shot Austin while he was at the pond." I watched as my husband collapsed to his knees on the ground near Austin, screaming, "No, I lost my dad and brother when I was four years old; not my son also! Please, God."

> "No, I lost my dad and brother when I was four years old; not my son also! Please, God."

Our two-year-old son, Dalton, placed his hands over his ears, screaming, "No, no! Not my bubba!" My father shook his head as he lifted up his bloodstained hands, trying to make sense of it all, and my grandfather was searching for the gunman through the trees. My husband heard voices through the trees and started running toward them, yelling, "Who shot my son? Who did it? Who shot my son?" I rushed inside the house to call 911, bringing Dalton with me to keep him protected from the gunman located outside our house.

## 911 Recording

Renee (screaming as phone was ringing): Oh Lord, help us…help us! No! No!
Operator: Noble 911
Renee: Oh, please help us (gave address). Someone just shot my son, and we think he's dead.
Operator: Okay, is there anyone there right now?
Renee: Yes, my five-year-old son got shot.
Operator: Who shot him?
Renee: Someone for no reason…down at our pond out by our house.
Operator: You don't know who did it?
Renee: No, my dad took him down to the pond to go fishing, and someone shot him.
Operator: Okay, I am going to keep you on the line. Okay, ma'am?
Renee: Oh, God, help us! Help us! (speaking to our two-year-old son crying) Come here, baby. Come here. It's okay; it's okay, baby. It's okay. Mama's so scared, baby. I know you are, too. Oh, God, please help us. Hurry, hurry, hurry! Oh, God, please help us!
Operator: We're coming. Okay, ma'am? Stay right there.
Renee: Oh God…Jesus…help us! Come here, Dalton. Shh, please pray for your brother…please pray. Oh, God, no…please, no…no, no, no…please, Lord, help us. Help us, God. Help us, Jesus. Help us!
Operator: Are you still there, ma'am?
Renee: Yes.
Operator: Is he breathing? Is he doing okay?
Renee: We don't know. My dad just came up and told us that he got shot for no reason, and he thinks he's dead.
Operator: Okay.
Renee: Please hurry, hurry, hurry!
Operator: Okay.
Renee: Please send an ambulance now!
Operator: Okay, I'm trying to.
Renee: Oh, God, please help him…please.
Operator: Okay, just stay calm. Okay? We are sending the helicopter right now. Just stay with us.
Renee: Okay, please hurry…please!

Operator: Just stay with him. Are the officers there?
Renee: No...oh, God, help us. Lord Jesus, help us. Come here, Dalton. The officers are here now.
Operator: Okay, I am going to get off the phone with you. Go talk to them. Okay?
Renee: Okay.

I ran back outside, where I saw Austin lying in the back of my father's ATV. The ambulance workers and the police had arrived. I wondered how the police officers had gotten to our house so quickly; the police department was located approximately five miles from our home, and they had shown up only a minute or two after the gunshots were fired. My family and I began to pray for Austin. I then looked up, and I noticed two police officers who were just standing there, trying to figure out what to do next. At that point, I was in complete shock. I took my hands and shook one of the officers by the shoulders, staring at his gun and name badge. "You've got to find out who did this to my son! You have to find out who did this!"

He removed my hands and said, "We will; we will. We have a pretty good idea of who did it."

"You've got to find out who did this to my son! You have to find out who did this!"

"Who?" I demanded an answer.

"Don't worry about it right now. We have the possible person in the back of the police car."

"Who is it?" I demanded.

"Don't worry about it. We'll take care of it." Very rudely, the police officer removed my hands from his shoulders and said, "Get over there and take care of your little one!" At that point, my mind could only focus on Austin. I was in shock it seemed, so I could only dwell on one thing at a time. I ran over to where my son was lying in the back of the Polaris. His eyes were halfway open and drenched in his own blood. I was still speaking to him, giving him as much comfort as possible, praying for him, unsure if he could hear me or not. My husband had been praying for Austin, reciting a Bible verse over and over, hoping for a miracle to take place: "And when I passed by you and saw you struggling in your own blood, I said to you in your blood, 'Live!' Yes, I said to you in your blood, 'Live!'" (Ezekiel 16:6). We both had strong faith that God could perform a miracle right there at that very point in time, and we were so desperate for Austin to live. We would have done anything at that moment to see him survive.

Grandpa Jim took Dalton for me to his house while my husband, dad, and I all headed to the hospital. We rushed through as many cell phone calls as possible on the way to notify our family, but I was still unable to reach my mother. I needed her so desperately. Surely my mother would be able to make everything better or at least be with me to comfort me. She always had words of encouragement, faith, and hope. Thank God for my parents, who have prayed for me, supported me, and have helped me even at the lowest times of my life. My father told me that my mother was at the church for a ladies service. He hurriedly took Jack and me to the hospital and went to get my mother at the church, located approximately ten minutes away from the emergency room.

Jack and I ran to the hospital door, out of breath as we saw my sister, Michelle, who got to the hospital first. "Michelle, do you know anything?"

"No, nothing. I'm sorry." Tears were running down her face and ours, too, as she held us in her arms. Jack collapsed to the floor, and Michelle helped me to a chair before I did the same. She helped Jack up, and we all continued to cry. We were all in shock, trying to make sense of it all. I quickly approached the lady at the front desk, rapidly breathing in panic. "His name is Austin Gabriel Haley. He was shot in the head. Where is he?"

"I don't see anybody by the name of Austin Gabriel Haley in the hospital right now." She was shuffling frantically through the paperwork on the desk.

"What do you mean nobody by that name? The ambulance brought him. They were coming here. They should have already been here. They were sending him by helicopter."

"I will quickly make some calls and track their location. We are going to get a waiting room ready for your family."

Everything was spinning. I passed out on the floor. I must have passed out two or three times since I still remember only portions. The grief was too intense. At one point in time, I felt a wet washcloth on my forehead, and I heard myself moaning, feeling as though I was outside my body. I barely remember a doctor coming into our waiting room. I looked up. The room was spinning and it only stopped whirling long enough for me to see Jack grabbing the doctor by the arm, demanding to know about Austin. Jack collapsed over me after we heard the worst news parents could ever hear: "I am so sorry, but he didn't make it. There was nothing we could do to help. I am *so* sorry." We both sobbed as we clung to each other. No words could describe the horrible nightmare going on inside of us. We knew somebody had killed our little boy. I was on the floor, still sobbing, when I looked up to see my father and mother enter the hospital room. I could barely get the words out of my mouth. With tears streaming, I finally said, "Mama…he…didn't…make it."

> "Mama … he … didn't … make it."

Mama collapsed over my body, and everything went black as I fainted again. It was such a nightmare to all of us. As I came to, all the family was trying to comfort each other. I instantly glanced up to see my father drenched with Austin's blood from head to toe. I could only imagine through the look in his eyes and the tears streaming down his face what guilt and extreme pain he must have felt. Jack and I sat next to him on the couch. Leaning my head over him with my arms wrapped around him as tightly as I could, I reassured him, "Daddy, it's not your fault. Austin loved going to the pond with you." He put his head in his blood-stained hands and cried harder than I had ever seen him cry in my entire life. He then wrapped his arms around Jack and me one at a time. I could tell it brought a sense of relief to him that we did not place any blame on him.

Through the intense tears, he spoke: "God bless you for feeling that way. God bless you both."

My father began telling us exactly what happened on the dock at 7:42 p.m. He knew we needed to know every detail, even though it was extremely difficult to hear. "Austin, Dalton, Grandpa Jim, and I were all standing there feeding the fish; everything was peaceful and perfect. Austin and Dalton were rejoicing as they watched the fish come up to search for food. Austin wanted to catch one, so Grandpa Jim was standing behind Austin, helping put a worm on his hook, when suddenly a loud shot rang out.

"A bullet hit the water directly in front of me. Water splashed into the air. I immediately knew it was a bullet. It was extremely loud, and I felt the concussion as my pants moved. I yelled, 'Quit shooting. We are down here!' The hair on my arm moved from the impact of the bullet. I reached around and got Austin and pulled him really close beside me. I was looking to see if I could locate where the bullet came from. Dalton took off running and ran up the hill away from the pond, holding his ears. Grandpa Jim took off after him so Dalton would not fall in the water. Six seconds after the first shot, a second explosion rang out. It was extremely loud also. I looked over. Austin was lying on his side on the dock, sort of facing me. Blood was gushing from his forehead, and bits of bone and brains were hanging out. The shot hit him in the back of the head and exited his forehead. It looked like he raised his head and was looking at me as if saying, 'Please help me, Grandpa.' Blood continued gushing out of his forehead so badly. What could I do? I thought about sticking my finger in to try to stop the bleeding, but that would be in his brain. He just looked at me, his head slowly laid down, and he died as blood continued to gush out of his forehead in a stream as big as my finger. I felt so helpless. Grandpa Jim brought Dalton back to the dock, walking over to where his brother was lying. As Dalton stood directly over his brother, he had the most puzzled look on his face. Then he looked up intently, and I thought he was looking up toward me. He just stood there with a look of awe on his face. What maniac was shooting at Austin? Since I am an attorney, maybe it was a client from the opposing side of a case. I do not know. I was so hurt and angry, and I still am. I am killing mad. I cannot figure out who killed Austin. I needed to get Austin to the hospital fast. I felt that maybe there was hope of saving his life. 'God, spare Austin,' I prayed. 'Heal this horrible wound.' After the stroke I had six weeks ago on June 15, 2007, I lost 60 percent of the strength in my right shoulder and arm. I was trying to pick up Austin over my left arm and held him in a bear hug. His little arms were hanging down as I lifted him in front of me. His blood was gushing all over the dock and me. It was running into my shoes and down my arms. I was desperate. Grandpa Jim was searching to locate the killer. I put my body between the place where we thought the gunshots came from and Dalton. I didn't want them to shoot Dalton, too. I held Austin over one arm and took Dalton by his hand with my right hand, doing my best to put my body between the shooter and Dalton as we struggled up the bank of the pond. I put Austin over the side and into the bed of the ATV. I headed for you and Jack as fast as I could. I thought, *How can I tell you, my precious daughter and son-in-law, that you gave me a bright, healthy grandson, and I brought him back shot in the head?* I was cringing with dread at the thought of having to tell you. I am so sorry this happened to my grandbaby. I wish it was me rather than my grandbaby."

> I am so sorry. I wish it was me rather than my grandbaby."

"Whenever I find out who did this to Austin, I am going to kill him. They used my grandbaby's head as target practice. Now I am going to use their head as a target."

Oh my, how hard that had to be for Daddy, and how angry he must have felt. We shared the same emotions. He loved Austin so much. I remember him saying on many occasions, "Austin, you are the apple of my eye." Austin had such a special bond with his grandpa and with all of his grandparents. Through the intense story, my mother burst out in an intense cry. I then leaned over on my mother. She pretty much pulled me in her lap, and we both continued crying uncontrollably. She said, "Baby, if I could take any of your pain away right now, I would." I realized she had her own pain, too. She also loved Austin with all of her heart. We simply could not fathom the loss of Austin; it hurt so much. We knew there would be a void in our lives forever without him. My mother-in-law, Bettie, was also brokenhearted. I knew she understood the pain because she had experienced great loss, also. It was almost as if she were reliving the moment from over thirty years ago when she lost her husband and her fifteen-year-old son in one tragic car accident, being left with eight other children to raise alone. While comforting us, she said, "I have prayed ever since Jack's dad and brother passed away that this would not happen to any more of our family. I just don't understand. Why?" Throughout the hours of grief and misery, we still had a very important unanswered question that we were discussing, something that continued haunting us: "Who killed Austin? Who killed our baby?"

> "Who killed Austin? Who killed our baby?"

We were still at the hospital. We had been there for almost three hours, and we still had not received any information as to who shot and killed our son. Our family was discussing every possible situation. Who was angry enough with us to kill our baby? My father was an attorney. He mentioned it could have been a client from the opposing counsel who may have been angry enough with him to want revenge. He had experienced several death threats throughout his career. The turmoil of not knowing who did this horrible thing was beyond what anyone could possibly handle. The nervousness and fear were overwhelming. We were afraid someone was out to shoot our entire family, and we were still scared for our own lives.

At approximately 11:30 p.m. that same evening, the Noble police chief and assistant police chief came into the family waiting room. The police chief stood quietly for a few seconds. He pulled his hat off his head, holding it in his arms. Glancing at the floor and then to all of us, he said, "What I am about to tell you is a very difficult thing to have to say. We think we know who shot your five-year-old son." The anticipation of all of us was overwhelming as we waited for him to finish.

"Who?" simultaneously echoed from all our family.

"Unfortunately, we believe one of our very own police officers shot the gun."

"What?" echoed again across the room. "A police officer shot our son? Why? He was at the pond, not doing anything wrong."

The chief continued, "The police officer was called to a neighbor's house about a snake. He was shooting at the snake. The bullet must have traveled and hit your son in the back of the head, approximately five hundred feet away." The details of how this all happened still seemed so vague. *My son was shot because of a snake?* We had trouble reasoning all of it out in our heads. After three or four different scenarios of where the snake was located, a police officer finally called the people from the scene at the time and returned to us, reporting, "There was a nonpoisonous black rat snake hanging from a birdhouse in the neighbor's backyard. They decided the best method of removing the snake would be to shoot their gun. When the three police officers heard Renee's intense screams approximately two minutes later, two of them jumped over the neighbor's fence to see if there was anything they could do to help. They realized at that moment the decision they made in shooting resulted in the death of your son."

A few members from the family went to see Austin for the last time before leaving the hospital. As we entered the room where he was lying on the bed, he looked very peaceful. White gauze was wrapped around his head, so the gunshot wound to his head was hidden. Each one of us took turns kissing him on the cheek and saying our last good-byes to him. I laid my head across his chest, and he still felt warm against my cheek, but I could no longer hear his heartbeat. The silence was deafening. We weakly and tearfully began singing to him, "Jesus loves me, this I know." Tears were streaming down our faces. I thought to myself, *We sang this very same song not too long ago on the day of his birth.*

Two Norman police officers who had taken over the investigation knocked on the door to the room where Austin was lying. They wanted to talk to my father and mother in the hallway. The officer got in my father's face. He said, "You had a gun down there, didn't you?"

"No, I didn't," he answered.

My mother immediately said loudly, "Why are you asking him that? My husband goes to the pond with his grandchildren every day or every other day as enjoyment with his grandchildren. There is no reason for you to ask him that question."

The police officer replied, "Ma'am, ma'am, we have to ask these things, as this is a crime scene."

Mama spoke loudly again: "There is no reason to ask my husband that question because we already know who did it."

"Who?" the police officer asked. Mama and Daddy began telling them the names of the Noble police officers who shot the gun and killed their grandson. With that being said, the conversation ended until later, when they took Daddy in a room by himself to be interrogated. Why they needed to continue with the interrogation with him, I will never know. The police officer continued the prior conversation: "We have already checked, and you own guns."

He said, "Yes, I own some, and they are locked up in a gun safe at my house. Do you want me to show them to you?"

He then said, "You let people hunt down there, don't you?"

My father said, "No, I don't."

Then he said, "Well, you don't have it posted, do you?" as if to say that since my father didn't have it posted, he caused someone to shoot Austin. My father was devastated.

He replied, "I didn't know I needed to have it posted. We live directly inside of city limits where many houses are lined up and down the street."

That accusation caused my parents additional guilt and pain which was cruel and unnecessary. My father will never forget the officers accusing him of killing his grandson when they knew all along it was police officers who shot him. It was cover-up time. I will never forget my father saying, "Time for the boys in blue to cover up for other boys in blue." Police officers interrogated Grandpa Jim after they finished questioning my father.

Meanwhile, a nurse walked into the room where we were still sitting with Austin and whispered to us that we had other family and friends waiting to see us in the cafeteria. Jack and I leaned over the bed, giving Austin one more kiss good-bye on his cheek, and told him how much we loved him and how much we were going to miss him. We felt so lonely. We needed our son with us so badly. He was supposed to be with his mama and daddy, holding our hands. But no more were we going to be able to hold his hand. As my husband and I walked down the hallway, I almost fainted once again, seeing so many people waiting in the cafeteria, giving us words of encouragement and praying for us. Both sides of the family were there, along with many other friends. God bless our family and friends who waited with us until two thirty in the morning! Approximately two hundred people came to the hospital. I do not think anyone will ever realize how much this meant to us—we did not have to grieve alone. Jack and I sat in the middle of the room in two chairs, crying but thanking God for the five wonderful years we had with our Austin. Oh, how we were going to miss him!

The next step was extremely difficult. It was time to leave the hospital without our precious boy, Austin, holding our hand or saying the usual, "Mama and Daddy, I love you." Our hearts were broken. How could we go home? By the time we picked up Dalton from my grandma and grandpa's house, it was two forty-five in the morning. Chad, my sister's husband, had very kindly gone to stay with Dalton so Grandma Dixie and Grandpa Jim could be with us at the hospital. Our two-year-old, Dalton, had been asleep for quite some time, but he barely opened his sleepy eyes long enough to ask, "Daddy, is Bubba going to be okay?"

> "Daddy, is Bubba going to be okay?"

Jack and I cried again. Our hearts were so broken for Dalton, too. His big brother—his best friend, the one he laughed with, learned from, and played with every day—was gone forever. Jack whispered, "Shh, we'll have to talk about it in the morning." Dalton fell back asleep in his daddy's arms. We drove home and laid him down in his bed, fast asleep. As we looked around our house, we saw Austin's half-completed puzzle on the floor, his television turned on his favorite channel, his much-loved bear blanket exactly where he left it. How lonely it made us feel—how lost we were. But the hardest step was yet to come. The next morning, how were we going to be able to tell Dalton that his "bubba" was gone, out of his life, forever?

"Be merciful to me, O Lord, for I am in distress; my eyes grow weak with sorrow, my soul and my body with grief" (Psalm 31:9).

# Comfort Your Grieving Children

"Train up a child in the way he should go, and when he is old, he will not depart from it" (Proverbs 22:6).

"But Jesus said, 'Let the children come to me, and do not forbid them; for of such is the kingdom of heaven'" (Matthew 19:14).

The day following the tragedy was extremely difficult and very lonely for the three of us, including our two-year-old son, Dalton. Prior to the accident, the usual morning had always begun with Austin quietly entering Dalton's bedroom, making sure he did not startle his sleeping brother, lying beside him on the bed, caressing Dalton and lovingly rubbing his little face. When Dalton got up, Austin had always been there to help pour Dalton's cereal each morning after Dalton had gotten out of bed. They would snuggle up on the floor together with Austin's favorite bear blanket. They would turn on movies and watch television together until Mama and Daddy got up.

That day was unusually quiet. Dalton, almost three years old, woke up that morning not finding his Bubba next to him. It was as though he knew something was wrong. He immediately took his daddy by the hand, as his daddy was right there with Dalton when he opened his little eyes, and asked, "Daddy, where is Bubba? Is he going to be okay?" Jack led him to me since he just could not bring himself to answer his question as he was trying to fight back the tears. Jack stood behind Dalton with his hands on Dalton's shoulders to give him support, as we were now about to encounter the hardest thing we had ever had to do. I got down on my knees, tears streaming down my face, and I said, "Dalton, what I am about to say is so hard for Mama to have to tell you. It makes me so sad for you. Your bubba, Austin, will not be able to live in this house again. He went to heaven last night. Austin cannot come back here, but we are going to be able to go see him in heaven someday."

Those words had to be too much for his little mind to bear as Dalton quickly yanked back from my arms that had been placed around his waist, screaming "No, no! Why? I don't want Bubba to go. I need him."

I gently picked up my baby boy, sat in my recliner, and held him close to me. Both of us were sitting silently while tears were streaming down my face upon his little head. Dalton just stared at the wall with such deep hurt in his greenish blue eyes. I held him a long time. Neither of us moved; my husband, not speaking a word, was silently crying uncontrollably, sitting in the recliner next to us. No movement was in the room. No sounds from children laughing and playing. How could we live like this? Life had been changed *forever*. Helping my child through this horrible agony of losing his brother was not going to be easy. I loved Dalton very much, and to see his little heart broken was overwhelming me. Together, as a family, we took one second, one minute, one hour, and eventually, one day at a time.

Dalton saw his brother fall to the dock on August 3, 2007. How could we help Dalton through what he saw? Jack and I both needed strength from the Lord to uplift Dalton and encourage him. We desperately needed words to say to him and understanding on how to help our grieving child. There was absolutely no way we could have prepared for such a traumatic situation. When it seemed at times that all our strength was gone, we would continue praying. Dalton needed to hear how God was still the focus of our lives. Several times a day I would lay my hands on him and pray, "Dear Jesus, you see our child who misses his brother beyond words. Please help him, Lord. Give him peace and fill the hole in his heart with your love every day."

Many times, as Dalton would think about Austin, sadness would fill his little heart and he would begin asking, "Mama and Daddy, would you pray for me?" There was something about the name of Jesus! He would bring us peace even when we did not understand how that was possible. Even Dalton, at the age of two, understood that Jesus would help him when he became sad. One night I knelt down beside him, and we were about to pray before going to sleep. What he said next was completely unexpected, but it is the most amazing thing I have ever heard. These are the words that helped us immensely from our little Dalton the day after his brother passed away: "Mama, Jesus came and got Austin at the pond."

"What?" I asked. "You saw Jesus?" Kneeling down beside his bed, I eagerly listened intensely as he began giving more details one at a time.

> Jesus took Austin up, up, up in the sky, and he gave Jesus a big hug and kiss on the cheek.

"I saw a big sun (placing his arms in a big circle with his hands meeting way above his head). Jesus came down and put his hand out like this (putting his palm up). Austin put his hand out like this (putting his palm down). Jesus took Austin up, up, up in the sky, and he gave Jesus a big hug and kiss on the cheek. I told him, 'Come back, Bubba. Come back, Bubba!' Austin said, 'I can't come back, Dalton; I'm going to heaven, but I will see you there!" He continued repeating the same story the next day to his grandma as we were riding in the car together. Amazing! With no doubt, Jesus allowed

Dalton to see that amazing moment to help him understand what lies beyond death—to not be afraid. God most likely knew it was too much for Dalton to see his brother—his very best friend in the entire world—get shot and killed. Seeing Jesus that night with his brother in his arms brought comfort and peace to Dalton. I also believe God helped our precious son speak the story to us, too, so we would also be comforted. I lay across my bed that evening—feeling intense grief without my son, but comforted from what Dalton had just told me and began reading in my Bible how God will speak through the mouths of children:

> "Do you hear what these are saying?" And Jesus said to them, "Yes, have you never read, 'Out of the mouths of babes and nursing infants you have perfected praise?'"
> Matthew 21:16

> Out of the mouths of babes and nursing infants you have ordained strength, because of your enemies, that you may silence the enemy and the avenger.
> Psalm 8:2

> At that time Jesus answered and said, "I thank you, Father, Lord of heaven and earth, that you have hidden these things from the wise and prudent and have revealed them to babes."
> Matthew 11:25

Even though Dalton was comforted by seeing Austin in the arms of Jesus, he still grieved, encountered loneliness, and had to face many fears. Death is so difficult to understand for an adult, much less for a child. No one can prepare for the dark days ahead of striving to help their child after the death of their sibling. Our hearts ached for Dalton, especially the first few weeks. We would watch as he would get out the same toys he remembered playing with when he played with Austin; he would try to make-believe just like he did with Austin. We could tell it just was not the same. He missed his brother laughing or saying, "That is a great idea, little brother." Everything in the house became instantly quiet. No more giggling or laughing, no sounds of Austin's footsteps as he ran from his little brother from one end of the house to the other while playing chase, no clicking of the play swords between Austin and Dalton; no more sounds at all of the life we knew before. Everything became silent, and the silence was deafening. Every day that went by, we missed Austin more and more, but somehow we had to be there for Dalton. Sure, Jack and I were grieving. We did not feel like doing anything, but we would force ourselves to crawl down in the middle of the living room floor, sit where Austin sat, and try to play the same games we used to watch Austin and Dalton play. Doing so brought a little more happiness to Dalton's world and possibly a little more normality to his life. It also helped us remember many of Austin's favorite games and toys. Oh, how we long to see Austin and Dalton playing together again.

Many times we would talk about Austin's death for awhile, then cry awhile, then play awhile again. A child does not automatically understand how to deal with tragedy. They learn by watching others, like they learn everything else. The Bible says, "Rejoice with those who rejoice, and weep with those who weep" (Romans 12:15). There were times that I told Dalton, "I feel very sad because Austin is not here with us anymore," or, "It made me feel angry when Austin was shot." Dalton would respond with, "Yeah, me too." I knew Dalton was sad and very angry, just like we were. Who wouldn't be? He needed to know that it was just fine to feel those feelings. Children give back the amount of love they are given. On many occasions, he would see me crying while doing the dishes or combing my hair in front of the mirror. He would wrap his little arms around my legs and give me the most comforting words ever: "It is okay, Mama. I am sad, too." I wrapped my arms around him, pulled him into my lap, and gave him a very long, heartfelt hug. It helps, while grieving, to have someone else grieve with you. Children feel the same way.

The more Dalton talked, the more we understood his inner feelings, emotions, and thoughts. We realized that a little boy who was almost three could not possibly comprehend as much as an adult. However, we knew he had identical feelings as an adult. At times, the things he would say would not be easy to hear, but we still encouraged him to talk to us about it. We knew that if we could get Dalton to open up and express his feelings the best that he could, we as parents would be able to interact with him to bring him comfort through our words. We wanted him to understand everything that happened on that day. I noticed Dalton's memory was associated many times with colors: "What was that blue thing Austin was laying on when they put him in the ambulance?"

I replied by telling him the name. "A gurney is a blue bed that they lay people on when they go in an ambulance."

A few times he would ask, "Why was Austin so red when he fell on the dock? His arm was red, too."

We were very honest in telling him, "That was blood on Austin's body, Honey. Do you know when you fall and cut your leg? It bleeds a little, right? Well, whenever Austin got shot, it made him bleed, too."

Months later, Dalton had still not forgotten any of what happened on that horrible day. He was still speaking about his memories. "Mama, if I only had a towel that day, I could have cleaned him off. He would have been just fine." I explained to him there was nothing anybody could do to help—Daddy and Mama could not help him either. We wanted to relieve him of any guilt that he was putting on himself. Even children feel guilt when there is a tragedy. Jack and I reassured him it was not his fault.

> "Mama, why did Austin want to leave me and go to heaven?"

I was pushing him in the swing outside the house when he asked, "Mama, why did Austin want to leave me and go to heaven?"

I told him, "Dalton, your bubba did not *want* to leave you. He loved playing with you and being your big brother. But police officers made a very bad decision to shoot their gun. It was a bad accident." I noticed one question would lead to another. It was fine, though. I wanted him to feel he could talk to us.

He began asking, "Are the police officers going to shoot me? I'm scared of police officers." He became extremely terrified of police officers, trembling and shaking when one was even near. It is strange how a traumatic situation can do that. Every time we or any of our family members saw a police officer, we experienced such anger, bitterness, and deep hurt. These feelings were beyond what we could even begin to explain, as we knew there would be a void in our family that would never vanish. We could not help but to feel angry with *all* the police officers; we were a little leery of every one of them. Psychologically, it did something to our subconscious minds. I believe it was the symbol of their uniform—the badge, the gun. We had to pray about this daily because we realized that not all police officers killed our little boy.

Several months had passed when I saw two police officers at a restaurant in Noble. Without Dalton's knowledge, I went up to the police officers and told them of Dalton's fear. I asked them if they would get on his level and speak to him very kindly. When Dalton came up to them, these two police officers did exactly that. They knelt down, gave him a high-five, and spoke to him for a couple of minutes. It helped tremendously. His fears subsided toward police officers after that point.

However, I do not believe there will be a time when *all* fears will go away. For example, a year and a half after Austin passed away, I was telling Dalton that it was time to get our last set of shots before Pre-K began. Immediately, he sank back into the recliner, crying and shaking from head to toe. I was surprised at his reaction. He stood up and asked, "Okay. Mama, can I get one last hug from you? I will miss you." Tears were streaming down his face.

I then said, "Son, why are you saying that? We are only getting a sho…" I stopped. It broke my heart for him when I realized what he thought I meant. He thought he was going to get shot—like Austin. I knelt down, eye level, and reassured him that it was not a shot with a gun. I explained to him it was only going to be with a small needle that puts medicine in his skin. He felt much better after the explanation and said, "Oh, okay. I am going to be brave, then." He did great after that, and I told him I would begin calling them "immunizations" instead.

Children understand death at various levels, depending on age. We have several children in our family who dealt with Austin's death in many different ways. They all had many questions, hurt, loneliness, and pain. It was very difficult for all of them. I recall my nephew, Cooper, who had a fear of police officers. He saw a police officer and told his mother, "Mama, be careful! There's a policeman. He might shoot us, too! We are all going to die! We're all going to die! The cops are going to kill us all!" He worried very much.

> "Mama, be careful! There's a policeman. He might shoot us, too! We are all going to die! We're all going to die! The cops are going to kill us all!"

Shaylin, my niece, was only eight months older than Austin. They were extremely close. Rather than cousins, they seemed more like sister and brother. Shaylin had lost someone very dear to her. My heart grieved for her. At restaurants she would feel lost when Austin was no longer there to sit next to her, and when it was time to play, she felt very lonely.

Austin's friends from school all felt the same way—boys and girls alike. I recall visits from Austin's closest friends. They would say things such as, "He was my very best friend in this entire world," "I loved him so much," "Why does he have to be gone forever?" and "We always played together." Austin was blessed with many friends who cared deeply for him. Many times, I think of how blessed he was to have so many people who loved him. It just was not fair for anybody, including the little children who loved Austin so much.

Austin had so many "best" friends. Austin would tell me how he did not just have one best friend but rather, many of them. All Jack and I could dwell on at times was how unfair his death was to all of his friends and family. Austin loved them so much. Their world was turned upside down. I was concerned about all the children who were affected by Austin's death. At certain times, children need a Band-Aid for a cut or a wound; these children needed a Band-Aid on their heart.

I began taking the time to study how much children really do understand. These categories helped me understand what questions children may have, what feelings they might encounter, and how I could help them:[1]

## Ages 2–4 Years:

Young children may begin to understand the concept of death but do not comprehend how final it really is. Some may expect the person to reappear. They think in literal and concrete terms and will be confused by statements such as "gone away" or "gone to sleep." Children of this age may require repeated explanations of what has happened. As their thinking is very much centered on themselves, they may consider that something they did or said caused the death. These children need to be reassured that they did not do anything wrong—in short, simple terminology. Consider using "play" to show the child how it all happened if possible.

## Ages 5–7 Years:

At about five years of age, most children realize that people who have died are different from those who are alive. The person can no longer feel, hear, see, smell, or speak and does not need to eat or drink. By seven years of age, the majority of children accept that death is permanent and that it can happen to anyone. This can result in separation anxiety. They are more able to express their thoughts and feelings but may conceal them and outwardly appear unaffected. They need to be given an opportunity to ask questions and to be given as much information as possible to allow them to adjust.

## Ages 8–12 Years:

At this age, children's understanding of death almost matches that of an adult, although they find it difficult to grasp abstract concepts. An important factor is their deepening realization of the inevitability of death and an increasing awareness of their own mortality and the fear and insecurity that this can cause.

They need to know details continually for a while and may seek answers to very specific questions.

## Age of Adolescence:

The struggle for independence at this age may cause bereaved teenagers to challenge the beliefs and expectations of others as to how they should be feeling or behaving. Death increases anxieties about the future; they may question the meaning of life and experience depression. Teenagers may find it easier to discuss their feelings with a sympathetic friend or adult than a close family member. They may be having difficulty coming to terms with their own mortality, including those close to them.

Comforting your own child during his or her grief can be very difficult when at the same time you are grieving also, but I realized that our son Dalton needed love and support. As I returned to teach my sixth-grade students ten days after our horrible experience, my mind was not focused on teaching them English. Many times, I could not get my mind off what our family was going through. I would stop the lesson and share with my students what happened on August 3, 2007, along with the many different feelings I was still having, and the grief Dalton was experiencing.

Students were able to understand some of the intense grief my family was feeling by relating it to situations in their own lives. One by one, students would come up to my desk or speak with me in the hallway. They, too, were going through difficult times. No matter how big or small the problems seemed to me, I knew if they took the time to speak with me about it, it must be very important to them. I would listen very carefully to what they had to say. One student told me, "My dog got ran over this summer and died." I knew this was a horrible tragedy in her life. She loved her little puppy and played with him every day. Another would say, "I lost my father last year to a horrible accident." A third would tell me, "Our house burned down. My family wasn't able to save anything."

One of the hardest situations for a child to deal with, I believe, is when their parents divorce. However, so many people think, *It happens all the time. It should be very easy to get over.* My students' entire world was torn into two pieces—two homes. Tears would sometimes well up in their eyes as they gave me all the details. I hoped at that point that I was able to say and do the right things. Most of the time, I didn't say anything other than, "I am so sorry." I would wrap my arms around each one of them, sometimes crying along with them. I felt love for each one of these students. They may not have known it, but I was silently praying for each one of them.

Children go through so much and often feel left out, forgotten, and many times, rejected when parents divorce. Some experience difficult things when cruel words are spoken to them such as, "It is about time you get over it. Your father or mother will not be coming back to this home ever again!" Get over it? How can they just get over it? They love their father *and* their mother! Another student told me that after she watched her house burn down, someone said, "Don't worry. You'll just buy new things." The things are not what were important to that girl. It was the memories that she had with those older things. New things were not going to replace the memories. They would only help make new ones. I felt I understood what she meant. I thought to myself, *No baby that we will ever have in the future will ever replace Austin. Austin will be in our memories forever. Even though we will love the new baby and he or she will give us new memories, our hearts will still miss our precious Austin.*

Children must never be forgotten while they are grieving! We need to show them a godly kind of love. Changes can cause severe grief. Care for them and take care of each of their needs. Listen for real—don't just pretend to listen. What they have to say is very important. Focus and help them through their most difficult situations. As long as it takes, help them, pray for them and with them. *Dear God, comfort the hearts of all the children who are hurting!*

> *Dear God, comfort the hearts of all the children who are hurting!*

Many people have come to me since the tragedy and asked, "What are some of the things that helped Dalton through his struggle of losing his big brother?" These are some of the ideas we have found to be helpful:

- Talk to Dalton about how he is feeling
- Ask him to remind his Daddy and me of some fun times he had with Austin
- Answer his questions (sometimes two or three times in different ways until he understands)
- Pretend play—about the tragedy itself and how he feels afterward
- Write letters to Austin, laminate them, and place them on the headstone
- Have Dalton pick out a toy or another item for the grave site
- Draw pictures about what happened when Austin lost his life
- Release balloons to heaven after adding a note attached asking for the person who receives the balloon to call (We received a call from San Antonio, Texas, from a lady, on her birthday, who had received our balloon 450 miles away. The phone call brought us much comfort).
- Have Dalton pick out toys or objects around the house that were special to Austin and place them inside a curio cabinet for safekeeping
- Have him help us plant a tree, and Dalton can water it daily
- Light a candle on special days
- Make a memory box or scrapbook
- Have Dalton write a story about Austin
- Laminate drawings and letters and place them at the cemetery in a three-ring binder

I have come to realize that the struggles of a child will become apparent in the most unexpected ways after experiencing a traumatic event. Be assured, many of these will pass, but there will be times, a child will need more explanation. Be aware, be patient, listen to your child's needs, and focus on helping them through their problems. Be there for your child. Communication is very important.

> "But do not forget to do good and to share, for with such sacrifices God is well pleased."
> Hebrews 13:16

# Forgive

I was extremely angry with the decision the police officers made in shooting their gun on the evening of August 3, 2007. They took my son away from me and my family. Many times, I still get angry. It is something that I have to pray about daily and constantly ask for God's help and strength. Forgiveness did not come easy. I didn't naturally overflow with mercy, grace, and forgiveness after they shot my son. Many people thought I should have been able to do that since I was a Christian. They would tell me, "The police officers didn't mean to shoot your son, so you really shouldn't be angry with them. You need to forgive and move on." I would tell those people, "It was a nonpoisonous, black rat snake that was stuck in a birdhouse. It couldn't get out because it had eaten all the bird eggs inside, causing its belly to enlarge. It was no danger to anyone! There were many other decisions they could have made that day. Are you telling me that you would not be angry if they shot your son or daughter on that day because of a stuck snake that was not endangering anyone?" Sure, every member of our family was extremely angry! Thankfully, God gave us the right to be angry for a while. The Bible gave me permission to be angry: "Be ye angry, and sin not: Let not the sun go down on your wrath" (Ephesians 4:26).

Even Jesus was angry at certain times, as shown in Matthew 21:12: "And Jesus went into the temple of God and cast out all of them that sold and bought in the temple, and overthrew the tables of the moneychangers, and the seats of them that sold doves." My family will always be angry with the decision the police officers made to shoot their gun. What they did was completely wrong and ridiculous, but we know they did not intentionally kill Austin. Their hearts were not out for revenge or to cause pain to my family. The absence of malice or intent has made it easier to forgive the police officers for the horrible mistake they made.

It is not uncommon for Christians to have questions about forgiveness. One question may be, "Is forgiveness a conscious choice, or is it a feeling?" I believe forgiveness is a choice we make. Our motivation for forgiving someone increases with our obedience to God and His command to forgive. God instructs us to forgive as the Lord forgave us: "Bear with each other and forgive whatever grievances you may have against one another. Forgive as the Lord forgave you" (Colossians 3:13).

Another question may be, "How do I forgive when I don't feel like it?"

> "How do I forgive when I don't feel like it?"

We simply keep faith in God. No matter how difficult, we still must be obedient to His Word. Many times, forgiveness goes against our nature, but we must still forgive by faith, whether we feel like it or not. By putting our trust completely in God, He will do a mighty work in us that needs to be done in order for true forgiveness to be complete. I believe God honors our desire to please Him and our commitment to obey Him. It begins with small steps—reading the Bible, praying, and growing closer to Him each and every day. Our heart, full of anger, strife, and bitterness, begins to somehow change to a heart more like the Lord if we will simply grow closer to Him. He completes the work in His time. Forgiving by faith is our job until the work of forgiveness, the Lord's job, is done in our hearts.

"He who began a good work in you will perform it until the day of Jesus Christ" (Philippians 1:6).

A third question Christians may have is, "How will we know if we have truly forgiven?" We will know the work of forgiveness is complete when we experience the freedom that comes as a result. God lifts us out of the bondage and sets us free of the burden from holding a grudge. Once a person truly forgives, the Lord sets him or her free of bitterness, resentment, and hurt that previously had a stronghold on our lives. Many times, forgiveness is a very slow process. It will come, but only if you allow it to.

"Then Peter came to Jesus and asked, 'Lord, how many times shall I forgive my brother when he sins against me?' 'Up to seven times?' Jesus answered, 'I tell you, not seven times, but seventy times seven'" (Matthew 18:21–22).

Jesus' answer makes it clear that forgiveness is not easy for us. Forgiveness is sometimes a daily occurrence and a conscious choice. Forgiveness may require a lifetime of forgiving, but it is important to the Lord. We must continue forgiving until everything becomes settled in our heart.

"Why do we have to forgive," may also be a question that many believers encounter. The best reason to forgive is because Jesus commanded us to forgive. We learn from Scripture that if we don't forgive, neither will we be forgiven: "For if you forgive men when they sin against you, your heavenly Father will also forgive you. But if you do not forgive men their sins, your Father will not forgive your sins" (Matthew 6:14–16). The Lord notices when we put out the effort to forgive. In return, I believe many blessings will follow. He cares for us and loves us. He desires for us to be close to him. "And when you stand praying, if you hold anything against anyone, forgive him, so that your Father in heaven may forgive you your sins" (Mark 11:25).

Finally, we forgive out of obedience to the Lord. It is a choice, a decision we make. As we forgive, we will begin to realize it is for our own good, and we receive the reward of forgiveness, which is freedom.

Seven months after the horrible, unimaginable tragedy, we had the opportunity to tell the police officer who shot our son that we had forgiven him. It wasn't easy. When we saw the police officer in the hallway outside of the courtroom; I had an immediate decision to make. Should I tell him how cruel and heartless he was when he took my son away from me, or should I forgive him and try to lay down the burdens of anger I was carrying toward him? There was a *decision* that I had to make—right at that moment.

I could not carry the huge burden of that intense anger any longer. I could only think of what Jesus said when he was facing the hardest trial he had ever gone through. *Jesus was hanging on that cross with nails through his hands and feet, he had a crown of thorns on his head, he had been spit on, blood was gushing from his body, and he was being cursed and persecuted. It must have been so difficult for him to take all of the pain emotionally and physically, but he still said, "Father, forgive them, for they know not what they do."*

Ultimately, we heard his cry: "I am so sorry. I wish I would have done something different. I am so sorry. No words could ever express how sorry I truly am." He was noticeably distraught and had lost a lot of weight since the tragedy. We could tell that he was truly apologetic. Jack and I both had tears streaming down our faces. Right in front of us was the very man who had pulled the trigger and shot our son. One at a time, Jack and I reached out to him, gave him a hug, and told him, "We forgive you. We will be praying for you." I don't know how. It had to be God helping us. The hatred and bitterness we had toward that man was somehow vanishing at that very moment. We'll never be okay with the decision that was made that day, but we had forgiven him, and we hope that God has somehow given him comfort also.

So, whenever I reached out toward the police officer that day, giving him a hug, I felt it was as if I was saying in all of my grief and at the most difficult time in my life, "I know you did not shoot my son intentionally. I know it was not in your heart to take him away from his daddy, his little brother, and me. I forgive you. I will no longer carry the burden of the intense anger I was feeling."

To this day I still think about how it felt to finally forgive the police officer. After losing Austin, I was sinking into a deep depression. I was sad and grieving. I was lonely and troubled. But, the worst feeling of all must have been the anger I was carrying inside my heart. It was a huge weight on my shoulders that I had to carry around with all the other feelings I experienced after the death of my first-born son. Immediately after that encounter, I felt lighter. I knew I had done the right thing. God began the healing process at that moment. It will always be an act of *daily* forgiveness I have toward the police officers; it is not always easy, but each and every day I pray for strength from the Lord, and I pray for a heart like Jesus.

"The Lord is a refuge for the oppressed, a stronghold in times of trouble" (Psalm 9:9).

# Keep the Faith

"The Lord will also be a refuge for the oppressed, a refuge in times of trouble" (Psalm 9:9).

Faith in God was the only way we were able to cope after losing Austin. The very second we knew Austin did not make it and his soul went to be with the Lord, a part of us went with him. Day by day, I would do my best to accomplish the simplest tasks of washing dishes, laundry, etc. Every task was misery. I knew every time I cleaned I was washing away Austin's scent from his clothes or his fingerprints from a mirror. I felt I was losing every part of him. At times, I would feel I was on the verge of losing my mind. When I gave birth to Austin, a perfectly healthy baby, I already had dreams for his future.

> When I gave birth to Austin, a perfectly healthy baby, I already had dreams for his future.

What kind of boy would he grow up to be? I couldn't wait to see him grow from being a baby to one day graduating from high school, college, and eventually having a career. What would his occupation be? Whom would he marry? What would my grandchildren be like? The list went on and on. My dreams were shattered, torn from my mind. There were no more "What is he going to be able to do next" questions. There were no more memories to make. His life abruptly came to an end so unfairly! At times, my heart could not take the pain. I would be loading the dishes in the dishwasher. I would see his little teeth marks on one of the plastic cups he drank from and had tossed into the sink, and I would lean over the kitchen counter and sob uncontrollably. Other times, while my husband would be driving, I would reach my hand back behind me to hold Austin's hand like before, and he would not be there. I long for the moment to hold his little hand in mine again.

Teaching school enabled me to keep my mind busy, but when I drove home at the end of the day into our driveway, life would slap me in the face. Many times after getting out of the car, I would literally fall to my hands and knees on the sidewalk, crying in agony. I do not know how long I would be there before I could finally gain strength to pull myself up and go into the house. Grief hurt so deeply!

The only thing that helped was placing my faith in God and His Son, Jesus Christ. I did not blame God. He did not and would not have taken Austin away from me. I blamed Satan. I was so angry with Satan for causing this horrible tragedy to happen. I can never have another child just like Austin, as God made him unique. No matter how many children God gives me, I will always love each one of them the same, but if one is gone, a mother will always miss that one who is gone. There will always be a missing link in the family. I miss Austin more than anyone could ever imagine. It hurts so much.

Although Satan fought me in many areas of my life, I continued growing closer and closer to God, as I realized at a very young age that God is my comfort and my shield in the middle of the storm. God became my strength and my guide. He became everything to me. Although struggles would be so difficult at times to face and I felt I could not go on, I would rely on His Scripture: "No man shall be able to stand before you all the days of your life; as I was with Moses, so I will be with you. I will never leave you nor forsake you" (Joshua 1:5). I felt the presence of the Lord after Austin's death. He was with my husband and me, helping us, guiding us, and strengthening us. *I will keep the faith.*

At times when I felt so sad, lonely, and depressed, I would put my closed Bible in my hands, close my eyes, and pray, "God, you know how I am feeling right now. I feel that I cannot go on. My world has been shattered. Lord, please speak to me through your Word. Somehow, someway, help me, Lord."

> Lord, please speak to me through your Word. Somehow, someway, help me, Lord."

I remembered a specific verse that helped me so much in my despair: "I have fought the good fight, I have finished the race, I have kept the faith" (2 Timothy 4:7).

I realized that living in this world is not easy at times. Christians will face the same struggles and trials as non-Christians. They are not exempt from trials, but they have Jesus to lean on during their trials and tribulations. My son is now gone. I have been facing a major struggle and trial, but I have decided to fight the good fight, finish the course, and keep the faith no matter how hard the struggles seem to be. Satan would like it if I got angry with God and turned from Him. I realized if I did that, Satan wins the race, not me! At times, I felt the race would slow way down, especially after losing Austin. I felt that I could barely put one foot in front of the other, but I would make myself somehow keep moving closer and closer to God. I will always serve God. No matter what life brings my way, I will always love him with all of my heart. *I will keep the faith.*

For some time after the tragic death of my son, I could barely cope. There was no way I could think about the long term of having to live without Austin forever. Instead, I would make myself focus on much shorter periods of time, beginning with a few minutes, and eventually building from there. The life of a Christian is not always going to be easy. There will be difficult trials that come our way at times. That's when we need to completely dwell on reading the Bible. It is highly critical that we allow God's Word to give direction in our lives while God speaks peace and comfort to us.

In order to help increase my faith in God to a higher level, I would read in my Bible the book of Job because I realize Job's faith was tested beyond what anyone could stand, yet he kept his faith in God. I lost my son—Job lost everything! His oxen and camels were stolen; fire fell from the sky and burned up his sheep and servants; his children were *all* killed; Satan afflicted Job with painful sores from the top of his head down to his feet. I can only imagine how much heartache and pain Job was going through. His three friends began with the right attitude toward helping Job through the grief. They sat with him for seven days and seven nights. No one said a word because they saw how much he was suffering. People find much comfort in knowing their friends are right by their side. Later, it must have been difficult for Job to listen to his friends question him as if he had already done something wrong. "What have you done?" they asked Job. Things happen in life that we don't understand. It does not mean that you have done something wrong. People go through various problems in life—even Christians—and even Jesus faced many trials and tribulations in His lifetime. "Man who is born of woman is of few days and full of trouble" (Job 14:1).

Each and every person on this earth encounters various problems in his or her life. Job explained his heartache and pain: "What I feared has come upon me. I have no peace, no quietness; I have no rest, but only turmoil." I related to this statement. It was difficult to find peace and comfort. The grief was too intense. However, I just kept thinking, *If Job can go through all of this and still not sin against God or blame him, can't I do the same?* "Lord, help me to keep my faith in you," I prayed repeatedly. By the Grace of God, I will keep the faith.

> "Lord, help me to keep my faith in you," I prayed repeatedly. *By the Grace of God, I will keep the faith.*

There are many different types of struggles that people face. Many times, difficult things can come across our path that we just absolutely don't understand. We ask, "Why me?" I cannot imagine trials and tribulations that you may be trying your hardest to endure right now. Do your best to think on the good things of life. Lift up your shield of faith, even when you get knocked down. Keep your

Faith in God; don't ever lose hope because there is light at the end of every tunnel. God will see you through. Remember: *keep the faith*!

"Come to Me, all you who labor and are heavy laden, and I will give you rest. Take My yoke upon you and learn from Me, for I am gentle and lowly in heart, and you will find rest for your souls. For My yoke is easy and My burden is light" (Matthew 11:28–30).

# Allow Yourself Time to Grieve

Coping with grief is a natural reaction to loss. We grieved so much after Austin's death—beyond what any words could ever express. Losing a very close loved one, especially a child you gave birth to, is beyond what anyone can stand. It is probably the hardest grief of all to deal with. Many times, a person will experience all kinds of different emotions such as shock, anger, or guilt. Sometimes, you may feel the sadness will never go away. These feelings are overwhelming, but they are normal reactions. There is no right or wrong way to grieve.

Many people would ask Jack and me how we were doing it. They said that it seemed we were going through the grieving process so easily. Well, it wasn't easy. When we got home from work, it seemed all we could do was cry. We didn't want to eat or sleep. Really, we didn't feel like doing anything. Jack and I both felt wounded physically and emotionally. A wound on the outside of a person's body hurts, but the wound on my heart was much more painful. During the grieving process, right after the tragedy of losing our son, it may not have taken over a second for me to encounter a much different feeling: sadness. After that, I would be confused. It was a vicious cycle that I felt would never stop. How could this happen to our family?

> How could this happen to our family?

My heart was shattered. I felt lost and alone. The grief was devastatingly intense. At times I felt I could barely function on everyday tasks. Believe it or not, brushing my teeth or combing my hair became such a difficult task. I would be getting ready and have to sit everything down, cry a while—a long while—and then try again. I literally felt I just could not go on.

In the mornings before teaching school, I would walk by Austin's bedroom door and realize I couldn't wake him up for daycare. My baby wasn't there anymore. I didn't know what I was going to do. I would feel my knees buckle as I would enter his room and stare at his empty bed. My heart longed for him to be there. Nothing—absolutely nothing or no one—was going to be able to take away the pain except for God. I needed him back in my arms where he was supposed to be—with me. Sure, I knew that Austin was safe and happy in heaven. It helped to know that he was not in pain. It helped to know that there were no tears in heaven. I wouldn't want him to feel the same sadness I was feeling. It was too intense. No one should have to feel that way. Later, my husband was glancing in Austin's bedroom and looked down at the floor. He noticed his laundry. He didn't care if they were dirty or not. It was his son's dirt, and his scent was on them. I recall Jack lifting them up to his nose, realizing his scent would not be in our house much longer, and he would lie across Austin's bed, crying. Jack and I would clutch each other in our arms and cry. We would cry out, "Why, God? Why us?"

Due to various circumstances and factors to be taken into consideration, not every person will grieve in the same way. Personality type, in addition to the way a person copes with everyday life circumstances, is to be considered. Above all, no matter which level of grief you may encounter, keep your faith in God! The process of grief will take time until a healing process gradually begins to take place. No two people will grieve in the same way; some may grieve longer than others. Ignore people who say "You should be over it by now;" they must not have experienced such a traumatic ordeal. There is no time limit for how long grief should take. Actually, I am not sure if grief *ever* ends completely—my grief hasn't ended completely. There will be times, especially writing this book, where I have tears rolling down my cheeks. Something that I hear, see, or do will sometimes

## Allow Yourself Time to Grieve

trigger memories of my little boy whom I love. I will ache for him and long for him just as I did in those first few days I had to spend without him by my side. Some people begin feeling better in weeks or months, and others will be grieving for years to come.

I overheard someone say, "The pain will go away faster if you ignore it." Trying to ignore the pain makes it resurface repeatedly and will only make it worse in the future. In order to really begin healing, you must face the grief. Thinking about it and talking about it with someone who really cares seems to help. I could not have faced this tragedy alone. It was and is definitely difficult to have to think about living life without Austin. At times, I absolutely *couldn't* think about it, and I had to force my mind to dwell on something else. Eventually, though, I had to face the grief again. Someone else has said, "It is important to be strong in front of other people." Remember, crying is a very important part of grief. Feeling sad, frightened, or lonely is a normal reaction. My closest friends and family definitely helped when I explained to them the way I truly felt. I simply could not hide my feelings when the grief was so difficult to bear. Remember, family and friends want to help and encourage you in times of heartache and need. I have heard before, "If you don't cry, you must have not loved him very much." There were times that I would be in shock and could not cry; then there were times I would literally fall to pieces from grief. I thought, *What is wrong with me? I should be crying uncontrollably right now.* Then, a few minutes later, sitting at the dining room table, I remember crying my hardest cry ever. Family and friends circled around me, hugging and consoling me. Their hands wrapped around me consoled me. I was torn to pieces. My whole life—the way I knew it—was gone. One minute I would cry; the next minute I could not. Grief is like that—crying and weeping come in waves. Sometimes the waves of grief were huge, and other times the waves were smaller, but it was still grief, and it was extremely difficult. Still, everyone needs to let him or herself grieve.

> Sometimes the waves of grief were huge, and other times the waves were smaller, but it was still grief, and it was extremely difficult.

In 1969, psychiatrist Elisabeth Kubler-Ross introduced what became known as the five stages of grief. These stages of grief were based on patients of hers who were facing terminal illness. However, many people have generalized these five stages of grief throughout other types of losses or life changes that may affect a person negatively.

## The Five Stages of Grief

1. Denial: "This can't be happening to me."
2. Anger: "Why is this happening? Who is to blame?"
3. Bargaining: "Make this not happen, and in return I will…"
4. Depression: "I'm too sad to do anything."
5. Acceptance: "I'm at peace with what happened."

As I dwelled on my experiences while facing the above listed stages throughout the loss of my little son, I realized these steps did not come in a certain order. According to Kubler-Ross, the stages listed above may or may not fall in order as we grieve. Actually, at this point, I feel that I will never get to stage five, accepting the fact that Austin is gone. I will never have peace about what happened on that August, Friday evening. She later stated in her last book in 2004, "These were never meant to help tuck messy emotions into neat packages. They are responses to loss that many people have, but there is not a typical response to loss, as there is no typical loss." My husband, family members, and I have experienced grief very similar to a roller coaster; it has been full of ups and downs, highs and lows. The roller-coaster ride has been extremely difficult, especially right after the initial unexplainable tragedy of losing our son. As the lonesome days go by, the grief has become less intense and shorter, but the ride will never ever end completely—it still goes on. Even years after our loss, we will probably still experience difficult times. The heartache of losing our son in death will never go away.

Many questions entered my mind as I was facing a nightmare of unimaginable grief. It did not matter which way I turned, I just could not find any consolation anywhere, but somehow God's Word helped to enlighten the ever-so-dark pathway that has been such a long road. I have so many questions that I will never get answered. Some of the main questions that have entered my mind are as follows:

1. Why?

    Why did the police officers decide to shoot a gun in a very rural area inside the city limits at a nonpoisonous black rat snake that was stuck in a birdhouse—no threat to anyone? Questions such as this haunted my mind every minute of the day. There was no reason for it when they could have used other methods of removing the snake such as hedge clippers or a shovel that happened to be next to their feet when they shot the gun. Why did the bullet travel the direction it did to hit my son at 510 feet away from where the gun was shot? I don't know. There were so many things that caused it to happen. Noble, Oklahoma, had a record amount of rainfall during the summer of 2007, so the dock where my son happened to be standing at the time was raised higher than normal. There was no good backdrop being used for the traveling bullet, so my son's head ended up being the backdrop. Why couldn't they have shot at a slightly different angle? They should not have shot at all. Why couldn't my son have been kneeling down feeding the fish food rather than standing? Why did God not stop this from happening to us?

    > Why did God not stop this from happening to us?

    Asking ourselves why was very difficult because there were no simple answers. Beginning at the age of three, Austin began having nightmares of police officers coming to take him away from us. He would wake up in the mornings telling us about the recurrent nightmare: "Mama and Daddy, I had a bad dream again. You would be walking on the side of the road with me. Two police officers would be driving down the road. They would stop the car and get out; they would pull me away from you and throw me in their backseat to their car. I was so scared. I beat on the back glass for you to save me, but you couldn't catch their car. You tried, but you just couldn't. They drove off with me and took me away from you." We would try our best to reassure him that the police officers were our friends. "They will not hurt you. Everything will be just fine," we said. On that tragic day, police officers did take him away from us. Maybe not in the same way as Austin's continuous dream, but they did take our son from us. After the tragedy, I would ask myself, "Why did he continue having that recurring nightmare?"

Through the anguish and despair, we turned to God's Word to help heal our broken hearts. I remembered in the Bible where even Jesus asked God, "Why have thou forsaken me?" He did not even receive an answer to his questions of why. Well, not at that very moment anyway. Thankfully, some day we will understand. Some day, when we get to heaven, all of our questions will immediately be answered. As I was going through much overwhelming distress of not being able to answer these questions, I could literally feel the comforting hand of the Lord upon me.

2. Who is to blame?

Immediately following the shooting, I felt that someone should be blamed for this horrible incident. Someone took my child away from me! When we had initially thought there was a murderer out in the trees, we were all scared for our lives. We were very angry and hurt. It was a question that had to be answered, and we had to get to the bottom of it. Sitting in the hospital for nearly three hours without knowing who killed Austin was almost more than we could handle and completely unbearable. In some ways it was easy to blame ourselves. Why couldn't we have just played on the swing set for a few more minutes before allowing them to go down to the pond? Why didn't I say something to the neighbors (whom I later realized were police officers) when I heard their muffled voices behind our house? If I had warned them that I had family members down at the pond, there is a possibility they would not have shot if they knew someone was behind their target. However, I had no earthly idea that there were police officers getting ready to shoot a gun behind the brush and a few trees that separated them from me. My poor father really went through it with guilt, I am sure. However, Jack and I did not place the blame on him at all. We both knew he was with Austin, as a grandfather should have been, having a good time. I realized nothing any of us did was wrong and we should not place the blame on ourselves. Some people, when going through difficulty, will place the blame on God or others when they do not know whom else to blame. There is an immediate decision that people have to make when confronted with tragedy: should I run to God, or should I run away from him and blame him? It is a very serious decision that a person must make. If you turn away from God, you have tied God's hands. You will never find the kind of help you really need except through God. Please, run to God, as I promise you that He will be there for you during your time of sorrow with His arms open wide. "For the Lord your God is a merciful God; he will not forsake you nor destroy you," (Deuteronomy 4:31).

> At that moment in time, it felt as if God lifted me up and set me on His lap, wrapping His arms of comfort around me.

I remember when I was at the funeral home viewing my son's body, I lay on my back, crying. I told God, "Please bring me closer to You. Allow me to sit in Your lap so I can feel close to Austin once again." At that moment in time, it felt as if God lifted me up and set me on His lap, wrapping His arms of comfort around me.

Running to God was the right decision. If I ran away from God, I would have never seen my son again. I am so glad that some day there will be a time when I will go to heaven and see Austin once again. Our family will all be reunited together. That thought alone is such a comforting one. What a wonderful day that will be!

3. What did I do to deserve this?

This is a question we all encounter as we face unimaginable circumstances. Many times, life is not fair. As Christians, we will face adversity and difficult times throughout our lives. Sometimes decisions may affect others. Although someone else may have made a very poor decision and it affected us, we should not put the blame on ourselves. Many times, people struggle with tragedy so much that they contemplate suicide. I pray God will help the ones who may be struggling. Peace and comfort is found in the Word of the Lord. May the Lord guide you through this intense grief at this very moment. "The Lord is near to those who have a broken heart, and saves such as have a contrite spirit" (Psalm 34:18).

We need to give our problems to the Lord and allow Him to do the rest. It makes the difficult times so much easier. God is our refuge and strength. He will not fail us, even in our lowest hour. "Though I walk in the midst of trouble, you will revive me; you will stretch out your hand against the wrath of my enemies. And your right hand will save me" (Psalm 138:7). We will encounter many questions as we face grief. These questions can become very intense, but make yourself whole heartedly rely on God's grace to help you.

There came a turning point in my life. Rather than asking God why, I would begin asking God, "Now that this horrible thing has happened in our life

> "Now that this horrible thing has happened in our life that is so difficult to understand, how can you use our situation for your glory?

that is so difficult to understand, how can you use our situation for your glory?

I will never forget when that turning point took place for me—when I stopped asking God, "why" and I began asking God, "What now?" I had just gotten home from teaching my sixth-grade students. After I parked the car in the driveway, I got out of the car and every step I took on the sidewalk seemed to be extremely difficult. Burdens of life were holding me down. I could barely put one foot in front of the other. I began saying out loud, to make absolutely sure Satan could hear, "Lord, you know I am having such a difficult time. You know, I don't understand any of this at all and why this had to happen to our family. But, Lord, I want you to understand—no matter how heavy my footsteps are, with each step I will draw closer to you." It was at that time I began to cry, and I remembered this poem written by Carolyn Joyce Carty:

> One night a man had a dream.
>
> He dreamed he was walking along the beach with the Lord.
>
> Scenes from his life flashed across the sky
> and he noticed two sets of footprints in the sand,
> one belonging to him and the other to the Lord.
>
> When the last scene of his life had flashed before him,
> he recalled that at the lowest and saddest times of his life
> there was only one set of footprints.
>
> Dismayed, he asked, "Lord, you said that once I decided to follow you,
> you'd walk with me all the way.
> I don't understand why, when I needed you most,
> you would leave me."
>
> The Lord replied, "My precious child.
> I love you and I would never leave you.

> During your times of trial and suffering
> when you saw only one set of footprints...
>
> That was when I carried you."

I felt Jesus carrying me at that moment. It was as though the words were directly sent from the Lord himself. It was then that I fell on my hands and knees crying out to God. Peace began filling my soul and easing the pain. I leaned over and laid face down on the sidewalk outside of my house and I cried until I could cry no more. I said with a broken voice—one that you could barely understand—"Lord, I know you are carrying me—I feel you. Please God, help me every day to live for you. Help me to be a light for you—somehow, someway—Use this horrible tragedy for your glory. Life will no longer be the same again; however, use me, Dear Lord, for your work in my life." At that moment, my heart was completely available for the Lord. Whatever his plans were had become my plans. Sometimes my footsteps still seem heavy and I can barely put one foot in front of the other; however, I have peace that it is during those times that Jesus is actually carrying me.

I have come to realize that recovering from grief takes time, but it is so much easier to handle when the Lord is carrying me through it. When I get discouraged, depressed, and lonely, it never fails that I hear a voice whispering in my soul, "Don't you remember what I have brought you from? Don't you remember I will be with you always? My child, never forget my love. Please, feel my love. Focus on me, and *I will do the rest.*" So, I go through life focusing on Him as much as I possibly can. He will take care of my burdens and sorrows. When all I can do is stand...I stand...for the Lord is with me.

> Therefore I say to you, do not worry about your life. But seek first the kingdom of God and His righteousness, and all these things shall be added to you. Therefore do not worry about tomorrow, for tomorrow will worry about its own things. Sufficient for the day is its own trouble.
>
> Matthew 6:25; 33–34

# Recognize Bad Things Also Happen to Good People

One key to coping with tragedy is recognizing that bad things can and do happen to good people. If you face the unimaginable, it does not mean that you have some secret sin or that you are not as spiritual as some healthy Christian down the road, as some teaching implies. There are teachings today that say that if a Christian follows the teachings of these "super" Christians and applies the right, "super" recipe, no bad thing will ever happen to him or her. This is simply not sound doctrine. Let me assure you that bad things also happen to good people. For example, the great Apostle Paul faced adversity. Paul revealed, "A thorn in the flesh was given to me, a messenger of Satan to buffet me," (2 Corinthians 12:7). Notice in 2 Corinthians 12:8, Paul prayed three times that the messenger of Satan would be removed. But the Lord spoke to him, saying, "My grace is sufficient for you, for my strength is made perfect in weakness." (2 Corinthians 12:9).

> God promised us that His grace was sufficient when we are in weakness.

God promised us that His grace was sufficient when we are in weakness.

Paul went on to testify that he himself had been beaten with thirty-nine stripes five different times (2 Corinthians 11:24). Three times he was beaten with rods; once he was stoned; three times he was shipwrecked. He had been in perils of robbers, cold and naked and run out of town. He escaped by being let over the city wall in a basket (2 Corinthians 12:22–38). Of the twelve apostles, all of them were martyred except the Apostle John.

Yet, God is still good. We have not made it to our heavenly home yet. So often I have struggled with the questions "Why? Why us? Why now? We loved Austin. We attended church faithfully. We supported our church financially. We worked in our church, sang in the choir, taught Sunday-school classes, and worked in the nursery. We in essence lived the so-called 'faith life.' Why did this happen to us?" We may not understand, but sometimes bad things happen to good people.

As followers of Christ, we should always be ready to give a helping hand to those who are going through heartache and trouble in this present world. Isaiah 61:1–3 states the work of the Messiah:

> The Spirit of the Lord GOD is upon Me, because the Lord has anointed Me to preach good tidings to the poor; He has sent Me to heal the brokenhearted, to proclaim liberty to the captives, and the opening of the prison to those who are bound; to proclaim the acceptable year of the Lord, and the day of vengeance of our God; to comfort all who mourn, to console those who mourn in Zion, to give them beauty for ashes, the oil of joy for mourning, the garment of praise for the spirit of heaviness; that they may be called trees of righteousness, the planting of the Lord, that He may be glorified.

God's people need to pray for others who are in need of a healing emotionally or physically while encouraging them to believe that God will be there for them. Someday we will understand the answer to all of our questions when we meet Jesus face-to-face. I can only say one thing with certainty that bad things do happen to good people.

As you face an unthinkable tragedy, remember God loves you and you are never alone. Remember, one of the purposes of God's ministry is to bind up your broken heart. For the person who is bound in prison of grief, God has freedom—to give you beauty for ashes, to put joy and praise back in your heart instead of heaviness, and rebuild you into a tree of righteousness. God is the restorer of broken dreams and broken hearts.

Remember, it rains on the just and the unjust alike (Matthew 5:45). Do you recall the terrorist attack on the World Trade Center? Many of those hurt people loved God and were good people when they perished. Churches and church people are in hurricanes, tornadoes, fires, and wrecks of all sorts. I fully believe that it is God's will that we "be in good health and prosper as our soul prospers," as stated in 3 John 1:2, but at the same time, I know bad things can and do happen to good people. Good Christians and good people are not exempt from diseases such as diabetes, heart disease, arthritis, and so on. Some of them, unfortunately, get sick and die, while others receive their miracle of healing. We must exercise a prayer of faith for those who are hurting in this world.

When we raise our spiritual eyes to heaven, we realize we live in a world of trouble many times, but we are pilgrims in this world and are heading to a city that is not made with man's hands. It is a city whose builder and maker is God. That is really our home. He is going to wipe the tears from our eyes, as God promised in Revelation 7:17. I can see my precious little son Austin running to me and throwing his arms around me. It is a dream now, but it really is going to happen. He is going to heal my broken heart. I can only imagine the happy reunion in heaven along with other family and friends. After all, there would be no need of a tree of life in heaven if there were no death and tragedy here in this world. That tree of life has healing in its leaves (Revelation 22:2). Once we make it to heaven, we will be fully restored.

One of the keys to dealing with the unimaginable tragedy is to recognize that bad things do happen to good people. When your life is dashed before you, when you can barely put one foot in front of the other, have faith in God. Somehow God will bring you through the horrific tragedy you may be going through at this very moment. Remember, God cares for you and when you hurt, God hurts also. God will always be there when you call upon Him.

# Remembrance Photos

## Remembrance Photos

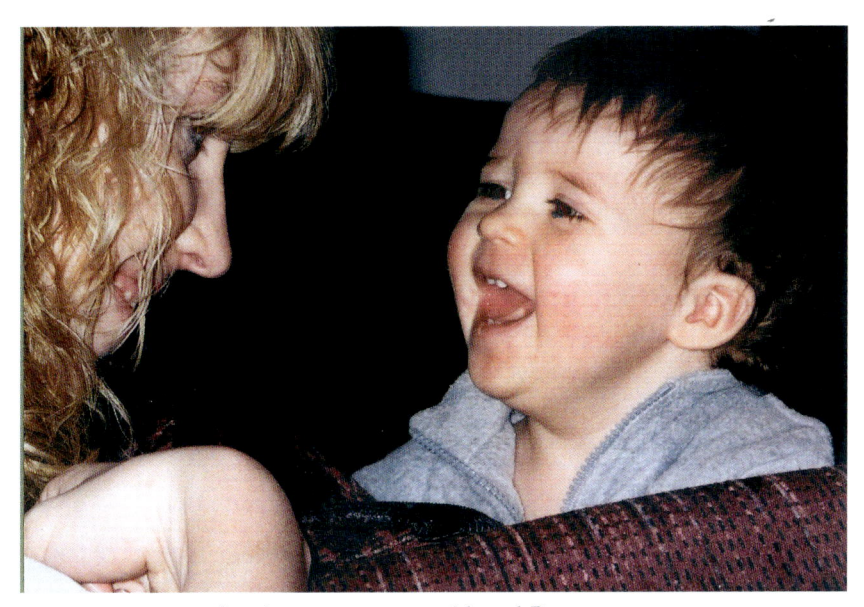

Austin was two years old, and Renee was making funny noises and tickling him.

Austin and Jack were spending special moments at the zoo.

Five-year-old Austin spending time with two of his best friends, Seth and Colin, after a T-Ball game.

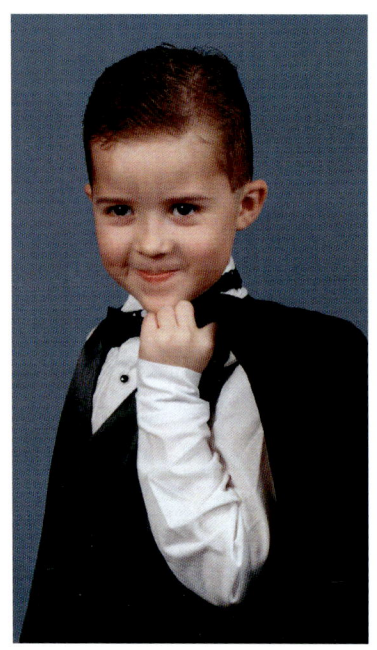

Austin's Five-Year-Old tuxedo photo was used at the funeral and on his headstone.

Even at the very young age of three, Austin developed a special relationship with his three-month-old brother, Dalton. (Christmas morning, 2004).

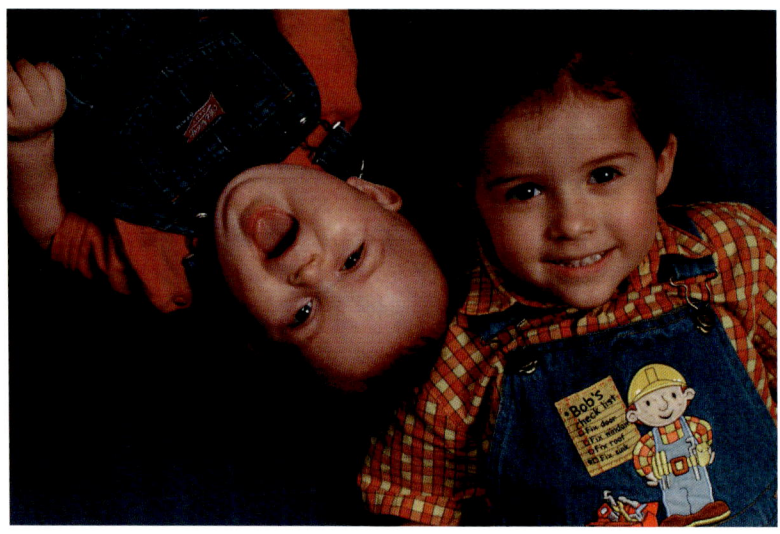

Remembrance Photos

Austin enjoyed every moment with his little brother—
even when Dalton crawled over him to wake Austin up.

The Austin Haley Story

Christmas 2006

Austin always enjoyed taking Dalton
for rides in his little Hummer.

84

Remembrance Photos

Christmas 2008

Easter Egg Hunt 2007 at Nanny's house

Austin's memorial on his birthday, Oct. 24, 2007 at our family-owned pond. Each balloon released from family and friends contained a salvation message.

Remembrance Photos

The black rat snake was hanging from this birdhouse when the shots were fired.

Austin's friends were still comforting one another even two months after Austin passed away.

Austin's Mama, Daddy, and little brother were holding Austin's treasured, camouflaged Bible.

Photo of Austin was taken outside our home while he was playing the game "tag" with Dalton.

# Give and Receive

"A new commandment I give to you, that you love one another; as I have loved you, that you also love one another" (John 13:34).

In times of tragedy, there is no greater gift you can give than the gift of love. This gift of love given to us in our time of need was a great comfort. Several words are translated as "love" in the Bible, but one special word in Greek is *agape*. We will always remember the love Austin gave us. In times of tragedy, we need to receive the love of people and we also need to give the gift of love to others who may be having a difficult time on life's road.

Austin was by nature a giver, and he had given to us so much. I remember and appreciate so much the gift of love Austin gave us during the five years of life. I recount those times when he sat in my lap and I read him stories as he looked at the pictures. He loved SpongeBob and other little cartoons about his favorite superheroes—Spiderman, Batman, and Superman. He loved to spend time with his dad in the shop. He wanted to grow up to be just like his daddy. And he really loved his little baby brother, Dalton. Austin hovered over his baby like a mother hen. He was quick to hand me diapers. And at times Austin loved to sit with a bottle and feed his baby brother. As Austin was a little older, he played with his younger brother and could not wait for Dalton to run and play with him.

He helped teach him to walk, holding his hand to keep "his baby" from falling. Austin and Dalton were completely inseparable—two brothers who were truly the very best of friends.

Austin's relationship with his little brother, Dalton, was very special. We can never replace the gift of love Austin gave to Dalton, but we also have our place in Dalton's life and can give our love to him. Part of the healing is the gift of love. I would hope that we all have and enjoy love—the pure love like God has toward us. Paul describes true love as the greatest gift of all. If we have not love, we cannot please God (1 Corinthians 13:1). Paul continues to teach us that if we have all spiritual gifts, all knowledge, and great faith and do not have love, it does not profit us, even if we give everything we have to the poor (1 Corinthians 13:2–3).

I wish we had a spiritual needle that could inject love into the hearts of the sad and the lonely. Paul described love in these words:

> Love suffers long and is kind; love does not envy; love does not parade itself, is not puffed up; does not behave rudely, does not seek its own, is not provoked, thinks no evil; does not rejoice in iniquity, but rejoices in the truth; bears all things, believes all things, hopes all things, endures all things.
> 
> 1 Corinthians 13:4–7

We should strive for this type of love. Paul continued by saying, "Love never fails" and concludes this chapter by teaching, "And now abide faith, hope, love, these three; but the greatest of these is love" (1 Corinthians 13:13).

**There is no greater gift than love!**

There is no greater gift than love! On August 3, 2007, our little son Austin, whom we dearly love so much, was lying there with no life in his little body. How have we been able to deal with this extreme unimaginable tragedy? The answer is through the love of God. We could not have made it without God.

I needed the gift of love from my husband. Many times, we

have held each other and hoped for strength from each other. Our love for each other, along with the love of God, has been a significant bond that has undergirded us with strength to go through this senseless tragedy. Without the love of my husband, I am not sure I would have ever been able to face the grief. We grieved together from the very beginning. We listened to each other with compassion, expressed our grief many times throughout each day, and we consoled one another as much as possible. When I was weak, my husband was strong, and when he was weak, I was strong. Marriages should never falter or fail during a tragedy. We should never place the blame on one another. At times, it is so easy to only focus on yourself during a difficult time of grief, but also try to focus on your spouse's burdens and do everything to help him or her through. I know my husband helps me on a daily basis, and I love him for it.

Also, I have needed the love of Dalton, our second precious son. When I have held him and loved him, I have felt his comforting love in return. In a little, simple way, his love is as pure as the love of God because his love is so true. The love I receive from Dalton, although he does not realize it, has been such a help to me through this difficult time of tragedy. It is astonishing how a small child can bring so much comfort. Many times, Dalton will give me such sweet hugs and loving words. He will come up to me, place his arms around me, and while looking so sweetly into my eyes will say, "Mama, I love you all the way to heaven and all the way back." Oh, how sweet those words are to me. He will give me a gentle kiss on the cheek. He is a very sweet boy, and I love him so much.

The gift of love given by the people around us helped to sustain us following Austin's death. Immediately after the tragic shooting, we were at the hospital. The love of our friends and family began to pour in. Many came to the hospital and were sent to the hospital cafeteria since there were so many of them. Some cried with us. Others simply sat and gave us strength by being there. We will never forget the love and concern shown by many of our family and friends. Many members of my family began to come in from other states. They all had some gift of love to give. Sometimes it was a memory of Austin. Other times it may have been a hug. No matter the type of love they showed, it all gave us strength to continue on.

We also received gifts of love from complete strangers. From the Internet came many kind things. Kathy Spivey took the photographs of Austin that were previously posted on the Internet from various news articles and altered them to put angel wings on him. Another photo was altered to show Austin looking up directly at Jesus with a large staircase entering heaven. It was beautiful. She also made pictures of the pond look so peaceful with an angel statue out front, and Austin sitting on the dock. As she continued posting these lovely pictures on the Internet, they really helped bring us a sense of peace.

In the days following Austin's death, we gathered at my parents' house near ours. Friends and church family began to pour in. They brought food by the load. We even had to get a second refrigerator and set it on the porch. We wanted everyone to have a snack and share the food with us and we needed their concern and love. Some sent flowers or plants. We received hundreds of cards through the mail—many from people we did not know. Some heard our story on the news and sent cards from the east coast and the west coast. We did our very best to keep a record of every single card, gift, item of food, and every flower. We wanted to send every person a thank-you card, as we did not want a single kindness to go without thanks. Every single thing brought us love and comfort. We were glad to remember every act of kindness with a thank-you card. Even though it took approximately a month or longer to write a thank-you card to each person who showed us love, we were glad to do it. We appreciated their kindness and generosity. We could not believe how much love and support our family received. It was wonderful, and it helped us more than words could ever express. To each of you who shared in our grief, we will never forget your kindness.

The day of Austin's funeral came. It was time to say our last goodbyes, a seemingly impossible thing to do. When entering the front doors to our home church, Noble Assembly of God, for Austin's funeral, our hearts were grieving more than words could ever explain. Jack and I could barely stand, much less walk, because of the overwhelming grief. We were still in complete shock and could not believe any of this was real. As we entered the sanctuary, we could not comprehend how many people had shown their love and concern. Once again, the gift of love was evident on that day. The entire front stage was lined with flowers and plants of every color; it seemed they were stacked from the ceiling to the floor. I believe every color that is in heaven must have been there that day. Our family broke in tears as we realized each one of those plants and flowers were a symbol of someone's love for us. There were so many people who attended the funeral that the church had to have an overflow room where they watched the service from a large screen. Over six hundred and fifty people came. We realized, then, how much it meant to have friends and family supporting us.

Words could never express our gratitude. Jack and I somehow gathered enough strength to speak at the funeral about our son and the love he showed to us and everyone else throughout his short life of five years, nine months, and ten days. Michelle, my sister, and Barbara, Jack's sister, did an amazing job telling about their memories of Austin and how he made an impact in their lives with his joy, happiness, and his love for Jesus. Pastor Dean, our children's pastor, had very kind words to say about Austin, including the moments that he got down at Austin's eye level and handed him the microphone to say his favorite verses on Sunday evenings. Pastor Dean and Austin always had something in common with one another; they often spoke to each other about—Superheroes. It didn't matter which one.... Superman, Spiderman, Batman. All of them were Austin's favorites. As Pastor Steve spoke about Austin's life, he also did a tremendous job, using an acronym for Austin's name to show the six things Austin would want people to know:

*A*–Always trust in the Lord (Even when you don't understand)

*U*–Use your gifts and time wisely for the glory of God

*S*–Show and tell your family that you love them every day

*T*–Thank God in everything

*I*–Invest yourself in others

*N*–Near (The coming of the Lord is near)

We appreciate each kind word and thought that was shared with us that day. It gave us strength and encouragement for the difficult days, weeks, and months to come.

Gifts of love were also shown by members of the community in a variety of ways. A few days later, there was a very kind woman from our hometown in Noble who heard about us losing our five-year-old son. Oh, how Laura King helped me during those worst moments of grief and despair, for she and her husband, Gary, had experienced a tragedy with their six-year-old son, Justyn. He was in a boating accident in the year 2001. Laura called me on the phone several times to speak with me after I had lost my precious little boy. She would sit and listen as I told her how much grief and depression I was going through. She would uplift me with these encouraging words: "I don't know how, but somehow and someway God will help you through this horrible time in your life. He will see you through." She began sending me letters in the mail that had verses from the Bible—this was so much help for my broken heart. Her gracious and comforting words would echo through my ears during the moments that I felt as though I could barely go on another day. Many times, I would read the same letter over and over. Then I would pass them over for my husband to read. About that time, another comforting letter from her would be in my mailbox. I saved each and every letter she gave me. When those times come, even still today, when I need encouragement and strength, I will read her letters. I believe that God sent her to uplift us. Her gracious kindness and love never ceased. She continued her support by sending me gifts in the mail. I still have a cross from her that hangs on my wall. As I pass by it each day, I read the verse inscribed: "Be still, and know that I am God" (Psalm 46:10). It brings such comfort, even almost two years later. I will never be able to thank her enough for how much she did. Her words strengthened me and helped me through. I was not alone—I had a friend who understood the pain, the turmoil, and the depression. I consider her a dear friend.

Jack and I often discuss how blessed we feel by the gifts given to us. All the gifts were amazing, and we will cherish them forever. The city of Noble named a children's water park in memory of Austin. We had several meetings and decided on the name of "Austin Haley's Kool Kids Splash" with assistance from Jack's mother who graciously thought of the name. It is such an honor. Throughout the summer months, I will sit on the bench at the splash pad and watch the kids play, including my own. Then I glance up at the large, granite plaque on the back wall of the splash pad, which has Austin's photo digitalized on it. Ada Custom Memorials designed it as a donation. What a blessing, and we appreciate it so much. On several occasions while the splash pad was in the process of being built, Austin would want me to drive by it to see if it was in operation. Each time we drove by, he recognized if the workers had completed anything new. He was so excited and could not wait to play in the spraying water. Not long before they completed the splash pad, Austin passed away. As I sit out and watch all the little children play, at times I will hear Austin's little laugh as if he is out there too. We appreciate the city of Noble for considering us and Austin when naming the splash pad.

Another honor was when a bronze life-size statue was created of Austin. Kim King, from the First State Bank in Noble, asked if she could donate money for the creation of the statue. With tears in our eyes, we told her, "We are so thankful for you thinking about us to this extent. Yes, we would love a statue of Austin." She immediately called John Gooden, a sculptor from Kingfisher, Oklahoma. He was excited about the project and did a tremendous job; the sculpture really does resemble Austin. It was amazing to look at it and realize, "Wow! That is a sculpture of our son." The statue of Austin will be sitting on a large granite boulder donated by Martin Marietta Materials and placed in the city of Noble as a peaceful memorial location. I am sure we will go often to sit by Austin's statue and dwell on all the good times we had with him.

About the time we thought all of the gifts were subsiding, Chris Rogerson, a music student from the Curtis Institute of Music in Philadelphia, sent us a letter. In the letter he stated, "I saw Austin's tragic story on the news, and it moved me so much that I decided to write an orchestra piece called 'Noble Pond.'" He invited us to come to Philadelphia and listen to it being played. So we did. In spring of 2008, as we were sitting in the audience and watching as the very talented orchestra played, tears were running down our cheeks. The music Chris composed was an outstanding piece that began as wind chimes representing a peaceful summer afternoon; then the music continued to build in representation of the tragedy itself. He definitely caught the emotions our family felt on August 3, 2007. "Noble Pond" was a wonderful gift.

Each person used his or her God-given talent and abilities, none of them being any less important than others, to help in our healing process. A letter, kind word, written song or poem, a gentle hug, the creation of special pictures and memorials all gave us strength. People should be willing to use their talents and abilities to uplift and encourage others who are grieving, as so many did during our terrible situation. All of the acts of kindness were a blessing to us and helped our broken hearts tremendously.

Ever since the tragedy, we have not only received wonderful gifts, but in turn, we also wanted to have a part in being a comfort to others. I realized how much it helped us to have gracious people who came along the way to give us comfort. So I would pray, "Lord, help me now to help others." Another key to getting over tragedy is to give love to others who are in deep grief—kind words, a hug, food, or a good memory. Because we had received so much love, we were able to give it in return to someone else in need. The Bible teaches us how to have compassion and how to give love: "Finally, all of you be of one mind, having compassion for one another; love as brothers, be tenderhearted, be courteous" (1 Peter 3:8). We have needed to give the love of God to others in their time of need. Showing others compassion and sympathy has been very important to our family. We now understand the pain that families must endure during a tragic situation of losing a child. The Bible teaches us, "It is better to go to the house of mourning than to go to the house of feasting, for that is the end of all men; and the living will take it to heart. Sorrow is better than laughter, for by a sad countenance the heart is made better" (Ecclesiastes 7:2–3).

When people are mourning, they need the love of their friends. It is easier to do the work of the Lord when people are hurting. To reach out to someone at the lowest point in his or her life means more than words could ever express. It brings comfort to know you do not have to face the lonely situation alone. Therefore, I do relate to this verse when it says it is better to go to the house of mourning than to the house of feasting. People who are sad, lonely, or depressed desperately need the comfort of others around them much more than people who are happy. A gentle hug or a prayer meant more than a thousand words to us after losing Austin.

> A gentle hug or a prayer meant more than a thousand words to us after losing Austin.

Since people had shown us so much kindness, we tried to comfort others who had broken hearts. For example, four days after Austin passed away, we heard on the news about a teenager, Thomas Glenn, who was run over by a truck. We felt so bad for Faye and Byron, his parents, and all of their family. We knew their grief was unbearable, as we were going through almost the same thing they were. Our hearts ached for this family. We seemed compelled to go to them, take them food, and express the sorrow we shared with them. It was such a blessing to give love to others in their time of need. I will never forget when we gathered hands in a circle in their living room and asked God to give them peace and comfort, to help them throughout their grieving moments. We continue with phone calls, e-mails, and going out to eat every once in a while with this dear family. We appreciate them being friends of ours. It is a special time when others who have lost a child or a grandchild share their loss with us. We knew when they told us they knew how we felt that they knew from experience and could attest to the fact that they really did know how we felt and that they supported us and were praying for us.

I continue listening to the news for parents who have lost a child.

I feel the need to call them on the telephone and do my best to give them a word of encouragement or sit and listen. Most of the time, I do not know these people personally. However, it gives me strength in my own life to help others in their moments of despair. Sharing my testimony of God's sustaining power builds my own faith and hopefully the faith of others. I can pray and believe that God will give them strength and will be faithful to help them through their grieving moments.

It is a blessing to give and to receive, and the Lord wants us to do both. The Bible even states, it's much *more* blessed to give than to receive. Every now and then, I get a card from someone who says they are remembering my family or me, and each one of them is appreciated. It brings a real healing to know our precious Austin still has not been forgotten. There is nothing better than giving and receiving the gift of love to one another. "Beloved, let us love one another, for love is of God; and everyone who loves is born of God and knows God" (1 John 4:7).

# Focus on the Good Things

"Finally, brethren, whatsoever things are true, whatsoever things are honest, whatsoever things are just, whatsoever things are pure, whatsoever things are lovely, whatsoever things are of good report; if there be any virtue, and if there be any praise, think on these things" (Philippians 4:8).

Immediately following Austin's tragic death, it was difficult for me to think of anything else other than how horrible the tragedy was. All I could think about was what Austin's appearance looked like after he was shot and not being able to live without him. The extreme anger captivated my heart and mind toward the police officers for making that horrible mistake. They did not only rob me of my son, but they also robbed me of my future grandchildren. Therefore, many things flooded my mind. The intense grief was overwhelming me. Many times, that black rat snake seemed to be Satan himself. The devil was having a great time keeping me down and discouraged. I could barely function mentally. My hopes and dreams for the future were lost when my son was taken from my arms, but while battling depression, I still had one objective in mind: Satan was not going to win and destroy my life forever. Satan was not going to win the battle!

As minutes, hours, days, and months passed by, I had to somehow, someway get myself out of this horrible spiral of depression, and with God's help, I would. So, my intentions were to do everything I could to make Satan angry.

> So, my intentions were to do everything I could to make Satan angry.

The closer I got to God, the angrier Satan became. He hated hearing me pray, so prayers would flow from my heart and mouth with tears running down my face, "Dear Lord, help me continue focusing on you. Help me, Lord, through this horrible grief and despair. My heart is broken, but you can make me whole. Even though I am weak, you can make me strong. Guide my footsteps. Send the Holy Spirit to give me comfort. Provide me with your strength right now. Lord, somehow use this tragedy for your glory. I don't know how, but you know, Lord. Touch lives through Austin's death." I knew Satan would cringe when I spoke about the Lord, so I would quote verses from the Bible while pacing throughout our home:

> I will love you, O Lord, my strength. The Lord is my rock and my fortress and my deliverer; My God, my strength, in whom I will trust; My shield and the horn of my salvation, my stronghold. I will call upon the Lord, who is worthy to be praised; So shall I be saved from my enemies.
> Psalms 18:1–3

> The Lord is my light and my salvation; Whom shall I fear? The Lord is the strength of my life; Of whom shall I be afraid?
> Psalm 27:1

Let me tell you: God hears the cry of a broken heart. He began giving me memories that were more pleasant for me to think about. God began helping me think of the good things about Austin. That became my strength. When I began sinking back into the spiral of intense depression, I would pray, "God, please give me another peaceful memory." He would bless me with wonderful memories of Austin.

Our five-year-old little boy was amazing. He was kind to everyone, and he had a very gentle spirit. He played with everybody at school and daycare, and he called them all his best friends. He was such a leader—it seemed as though kids just wanted to follow him. I remember when Austin's cousin, Shaylin, had a big birthday party. There were approximately fifteen or twenty girls chasing him all at one time. Giggling and laughing echoed throughout the gym as they finally caught him, knocking him down. He loved it. Then he would take off again, and they began chasing him once again. It was so funny because he really liked to be chased by the girls.

I recall the humorous times with our son. Austin never liked to get dirty. He always kept clean as much as possible. One time during the summer of 2007, we decided to go to my sister's house, so Austin and his little brother could play with their cousins. Austin and Shaylin, eight months apart, enjoyed playing in the sandbox. They would dig tunnels in the sand and build roads. Austin would always use the shovels, while Shaylin enjoyed digging with her hands. Austin decided he was ready to stop digging and began riding a small, motorized four-wheeler. He made a few circles around the yard on the four-wheeler, when he noticed Shaylin was raising her hand to give him a high-five. He reached his hand to hit hers, and then he noticed she had mud all over her hand. He hesitated on the high five, but too late—she gave him the muddiest high-five ever! He looked at his hand, wrinkled his nose in disgust, and said, "Ew!" We laughed and laughed because he wanted to stay clean and not get his hands dirty.

We would eat lunch at Golden Corral with my parents every Sunday after church. At the end of the meal, my father would always take out a dollar bill and say, "Austin, whose picture is on this one-dollar bill?" Grandpa had trained all the grandkids to say, "That is Grandpa's picture." Then my dad would let them keep the dollar. He never knew anything different, except Grandpa had a little different hairdo in the picture on the one-dollar bill. For all he knew, Grandpa's picture was definitely on the one-dollar bill. We had many wonderful and humorous times with Austin.

He enjoyed all aspects of life, especially sports. He played his first season of T-ball during the spring of 2007. He could hardly wait to have the opportunity to run the bases as fast as he could. He could run like the wind was carrying him. After T-ball was finished, he was really looking forward to football season. Austin only had an opportunity to practice a few times before the tragedy took place. I will always wonder what he would have looked like in a full uniform or how he would have excelled in the other sports.

Austin enjoyed many different games and activities. His favorite type of enjoyment was sitting with the family and watching superhero cartoons (one of his favorites) while holding his juice cup in one hand and his brother's hand in the other. When he was not watching his cartoons, he would practice putting together puzzles. This was one of his favorite things to do, beginning at two or three years old. Austin had a puzzle with each state as a separate piece. It never ceased to amaze me how he would gather all of the pieces around him on the floor and place them in a perfectly straight line with all fifty pieces; he was always very careful to line things up perfectly. He would tell his one-year-old brother at the time, as if Dalton knew what he was talking about, "Look, Dalton. This is Florida. This is where Mickey and Minney Mouse live. This one is California; Uncle Leonard drives his truck to California because he is a truck driver." He would go on, showing Dalton each puzzle piece and telling a little story behind each one. Dalton was beginning to repeat a few of the state names after he heard Austin repeat them so many times. Austin was so proud of himself for being able to finally complete the puzzle at three years old, and he had hoped Dalton would one day be able to complete the puzzle also.

Jack and I came to realize Austin was learning things at a very fast pace. Throughout each summer, since I was home with my children instead of teaching, I would really work with Austin on learning how to read and count. Austin was excited about it, and he always wanted to learn more. Sitting at the dining room table, he helped me cut small pieces of white paper into squares, large enough to write one word on each one of them. We found a variety of different words to write on each piece. The words ranged from one to four letters in length, and we completed writing over one hundred words together. I was helping him read the words as I would write them. Then we used each small piece of paper as a flashcard until he learned many of the words. Every night before I put him to bed, we would read through each flashcard individually. When he would read the word correctly, we would get a piece of tape and put the card on the wall to make a train at the top of his bedroom wall. By the time summer was about over, he had learned 110 words and he had reached the goal he set for himself. His goal was for the word train to line up all around his bedroom, and it finally did. I was so proud of him for accomplishing his goal, and many times I would swing him around and around as he giggled and laughed. It became a great memory, and I will never forget his enthusiasm as he said, "Mama, I want to learn another one!"

Not only was he beginning to read quickly, but he was also learning how to count as well. As we played on the swings, we had a routine of counting to one hundred. With each push I would count to the next number. Finally, after reaching one hundred, we would play something else. He really excelled in preschool, and we were very proud parents of a wonderful little boy. His fantastic pre-kindergarten teacher, Ms. Brown, was very impressed with his participation and ability in class, to the point of saying that he would possibly be ready to skip kindergarten and move on to the first grade. Of course, we did not get the chance to make that decision.

Austin ran everywhere he went; he very rarely walked. I always joked with him, "Son, you began walking at ten and a half months, and you learned to run the next day after that." He thought, for sure, that was when he learned to run, and I never told him any different. He loved sports. Austin, Dalton, and I enjoyed playing the game of "tag" around the yard while Jack was at work. Austin could run very quickly, and sometimes it was difficult to catch him. One of the sweetest moments was when he tagged his two-year-old brother, Dalton. I knew there would be absolutely no way Dalton would catch up with Austin since he was so little. Austin would act like he was running so quickly, but he would actually be running in very slow motion so Dalton could run up beside him, reaching out as far as he could, and tag Austin on his back. "Tag," Dalton would say in his two-year-old voice.

Austin would reply, "Oh, you got me, little brother." He would smile at Dalton and put his arms around him, giving him a really big hug. They always enjoyed time together, and our boys were already getting extremely close at a very young age.

June of the same summer, I took our boys to Vacation Bible School. Austin always looked forward to attending Vacation Bible School each summer with his cousins. That year, the different teachers had set up different rooms and a variety of games to teach Bible stories. I remember one of the games was an obstacle course. Most of the kids struggled somewhat in getting across the balance beam. The theme was supposed to teach the kids that sometimes struggles can happen in life, but we need to trust that God can help us. When Austin was on the start line, the teacher said, "On your mark…get set…go!" It did not take him over a few seconds to get from the beginning to the end. He moved over the objects, he dragged himself under part of the course on his belly, he went through the tube, crossed the beam, and finished the obstacle course in only a few seconds. At the finish line he said, "I didn't want the struggles of life to slow me down! God will always help me through." He surprised me when he spoke so "big" sometimes, as an adult would.

Austin was a very caring little boy who had a big heart. He would put others before himself even in the simplest of ways. For instance, the night before he passed away (the day of my birthday), Austin came to me. He said, "Mama, I really want an apple, but there is only one left. I don't want my baby, Dalton, to have his feelings hurt if he doesn't get one."

I said, "Son, I will buy some more tomorrow. Go to your room and hide. You can eat your apple in there, and Dalton will not know, so his feelings will not be hurt." That is what he did. I watched as he went into his room, closing the door behind him. I thought about how sweet it was that he did not want to hurt his brother's feelings in any way. He would always strive to please Dalton. After he finished the apple, he was then ready for bed. (Austin tended to choose very healthy foods most of the time. His favorite meals consisted of fish or chicken, apples or peaches, and broccoli. He always called the stalks of broccoli "trees." Amazingly, he never enjoyed cake or many other sweet things). Austin and I were talking about how remarkably he ate as I helped him get on his pajamas that evening. I gave him a small drink of water, and we were about to say his usual prayer when he stopped me. He said, "I want to pray for Grandpa and I want to pray for you, Mama." I thought how sweet it was that he wanted to pray for both of us. Grandpa had just had a stroke six weeks prior and was unable to move his right arm very much, and his entire right side was weak. He had also been battling Hepatitis C from a blood transfusion after he almost died from an oil rig accident in 1981. I had been battling physical problems caused by two earlier miscarriages. For a year after the last miscarriage, we were unable to have any more children and the doctors did not know if it would ever be possible again. Austin said, "I am going to pray that God heals your body so we can have another baby in our home. I wish I could pick out the baby." I acknowledged what he was saying with his childlike faith.

"Son, just pray and tell God what you want the new baby to be, and maybe He will answer your prayers."

He continued, "Well, I want to pray for Grandpa while you are in the room, but I want to pray for you after you leave." I thought it was a strange request since he had never asked me to leave the room before he prayed, but I said, okay. He prayed, "God, heal Grandpa in *one* day..."

After his prayer, I asked Austin, "Why did you ask God to heal Grandpa in *one* day rather than now?" He looked at me with surprise in his eyes, and I could tell he wondered why himself.

He said, "I don't know. I don't know why." After a few more minutes he reminded me that he was going to pray for a new baby in our family. We gave each other a kiss and a hug, he told me how much he loved me, as I did the same with him, and I left the room. It was the last night I would be able to tuck him into bed ever again.

Oh, how I miss those times, those few moments of just sitting and talking; those few moments of feeling his cheek next to mine and hearing his little voice say the words "I love you, Mama." I will never forget the way he felt in my arms and his sweet, tender voice. I miss him terribly.

After Austin passed away, Jack and I went into his room to search for memories of him. We looked for drawings or fingerprints. We searched for anything and everything that was a part of him—just something, anything. When Jack lifted Austin's pillow, he lifted up the core of the apple. He had hidden the apple, so his baby brother would not see it and feel left out because he didn't get one; there were no apples remaining after eating that one, and he did not want to hurt his baby brother's feelings. How sweet! He was such a very special boy with an extremely caring heart. It happened to be the small things that helped us focus on the good things.

Weeks later, we saw God beginning to answer Austin's prayers that he had prayed the night before he passed away. My father's strength began returning, and I believe God helped my father emotionally in *one* day—the day of Austin's death. There was a reason Austin prayed for Grandpa. Our little son may not have realized it, but my father was going to need a healing emotionally after the death of his grandbaby—not just physically. The prayer of Austin gave my father comfort throughout the most difficult time in his life. As months passed by, my father continued going to the doctor for routine visits concerning his Hepatitis C. His enzyme count before the tragedy were extremely elevated, but praise the Lord, now they are completely normal! I believe God also answered this prayer from Austin. I waited until I was closer to the end of this book to tell you the most amazing thing:

Nine months after Austin passed away, a miracle took place in our lives. We welcomed the birth of our new baby, Gabriel Jeremiah Haley, on Friday, May 16, 2008. We named him Gabriel because that was Austin's middle name, and his middle name is Jeremiah, after Austin's favorite verse: "But blessed is the man who trusts in the Lord, whose confidence is in him" (Jeremiah 17:7).

God is in the miracle-working business! We praise God for Gabriel every day. When he was born, we wondered if Austin went to heaven the night of August 3, 2007, and asked God personally for Gabriel. We like to think so. He has a very sweet personality and blond hair and blue eyes. His personality seems to be kind and gentle—a lot like the way Austin was. It helped Dalton tremendously when Gabriel was born. I believe God sent Gabriel specifically to help Dalton emotionally. After Austin passed away, Dalton would sit quietly, not saying too much. After Gabriel came along, we began to see happiness in Dalton again. He began smiling and laughing. At times he would say, "I am giving Gabriel a toy just like Austin did with me." He wanted to be a big brother just like Austin. Now I see Dalton taking the lead of being the big brother, and many times, he does play the same way Austin did with him. Dalton will hand Gabriel a little toy sword, and I hear the clicking as he and Dalton swing with all their might. Both of them will start laughing. They'll drop the swords and Gabriel will chase Dalton around the living room as fast as he possibly can, while Dalton sometimes slows way down and gives his little brother a big hug and says "Oh, you got me, little brother!" They will sit in the recliner together, and Dalton will pretend to be reading Gabriel one of his favorite books. One of their favorite moments together is jumping on the trampoline outside our house. Well, I can't say that Gabriel jumps much because usually it ends up that Dalton jumps and Gabriel typically goes flying on his back and hops up and down while Dalton does the jumping. Gabriel laughs and laughs. So does Dalton. It is so good to hear them playing, having fun, and laughing together.

While Gabriel has been a blessing in Dalton's healing process, he still has trouble with loud noises, and he covers his ears with his hands. Other times, he will say, "Mama and Daddy, I miss Austin *so* much," or, "When is the trumpet going to blow so we can go to heaven to see Austin?" I know he misses his older brother. He has a fear of losing his younger brother because many times he will ask, "Do I get to keep this brother forever?" Nothing or no one will ever be able to fill that

> "Do I get to keep this brother *forever*?"

void, but I am so glad that God allowed us to have Gabriel so Dalton can be a wonderful big brother to him.

We were so blessed with a final family photo with Austin included, although it was nine months after his death. Sue Elsenbeck, a photographer near our hometown, spent many hours recreating our family photo after Gabriel was born. She digitalized Austin directly into the photo. I have no words to express my gratitude for this wonderful gift. It gave us an opportunity to have all three of our boys in one picture. What a treasured blessing that was to all of our family! The recreated photo is perfect, and it looks as if Austin really is standing directly over Jack's shoulder. We are blessed to have friends such as Sue who helped us through our grief after losing our son Austin.

> Austin will never be replaced.

Austin will never be replaced. A piece of our heart went with Austin, and that part of our heart will never be filled again. Yet our hearts have been opened in new ways and to new people. Gabriel, Austin and Dalton's baby brother, is now almost two years old, and we are so blessed to have him in our lives. The love we have for him is truly amazing and wonderful—we are so blessed to be his parents. We love him deeply.

> A piece of our heart went with Austin, and that part of our heart will never be filled again.

Gabriel has brought us new happiness and joy. God is bringing us new, special joy through his role in our lives. We believe he is a miracle sent directly from the throne of God. My husband said having another little boy was a direct answer to his prayers. We remember that everyone kept saying while I was pregnant that we were going to have a little girl. But my husband just kept quiet while family and friends would talk. We both wanted a little girl and still do. My husband's prayer to God was, "God, please replace what was lost. Send us a little boy in Austin's likeness." At the twelfth week of pregnancy, we found out if the baby would be a girl or a boy. We found out that our little girl had yet to be conceived. It was a good feeling to know we were going to have a little boy. Although Gabriel can never take the place of Austin, his addition to our family helped us feel a little more complete. We still have hope for the future that someday we will be blessed with a precious little girl added to our family.

# Provide Strength and Comfort to the Grieving

Maybe you are not the one grieving, but you are trying to comfort one who is grieving. There are numerous ways to give support to others who are experiencing the pain of losing a close loved one; however, throughout this chapter I would like to also share with you some of the phrases that are better left unsaid. People should always encourage and alleviate grief. I truly appreciated the people who comforted us as we mourned. Thank God for family and friends who have grieved with us and supported us! Their words were like pouring healing oil to the very depth of our heart and soul.

> Their words were like pouring healing oil to the very depth of our heart and soul.

Even those who simply gave us a hug and cried with us without saying a word were extremely comforting because we knew they cared. People do not have the ability to heal all the hurt that a person may be feeling, but loving and uplifting words and the simple hugs were so comforting. While I was in the deepest depths of grief because of the loss of our son, just knowing others cared and were praying for us was consoling.

The following are some of the phrases that would be much better left unsaid when a person has lost a loved one:

- "I know how you feel": Most people probably do not know how it feels to lose a child in the same way that we lost Austin. I do understand that many have faced their own tragedies or have dealt with grief in their own ways and situations, although perhaps not one exactly like this. Therefore, at the time, and maybe even still today, it seems as if no one truly did have a complete understanding of how we felt. Most likely if a person says, "I know how you feel," he or she probably has faced a pretty devastating situation in his or her lifetime and is trying to be sympathetic, but unless a person has been through an identical situation, this phrase is better left unsaid. It would probably be much better to say, "I will never know what you are really feeling, but I know I can hold you up in prayer. You must be hurting so badly."
- "It couldn't have happened to a better couple": The person probably did not mean it in this way, but a card we had received from someone said this statement. We didn't quite understand this statement, as this tragedy was not something good that happened—it was a horrifying nightmare of a tragedy. We felt a little empty inside after receiving this card, as we didn't understand the meaning behind the words. Maybe it would be better to say, "I just don't know how this could have happened to you. I will be supporting you, and I am so sorry you have to go through this very difficult time.
- "He was predestined to die at the age of five": We do not believe God intentionally causes someone to die at any age due to predestination. We never blamed God for Austin's death, but we prayed God could use the tragic situation for His glory once it happened. It is impossible for humans to determine what God's plan is exactly; it is hurtful to insinuate that God would give us a wonderful son and then take him from us after only

five years. Instead of this type of statement, use comforting Bible verses to quote to the hurting individual.
- "Things happen for a reason": Pain in this sort of tragedy is too difficult to think there may be a reason for it. These words would be better said: "I wish I could give you a reason why, but there is no way I can. However, I will be praying that God brings you comfort and peace."
- "It was God's will": What does that make the police officers—God's helpers? It is not our belief that God intended for our five-year-old Austin to die on that day. However, God does not stop people from making choices. God has blessed most people with the ability to reason things out, hoping we will choose to do the right thing. He allows the freewill of people. People are free moral agents. God allows people to make choices, whether good or bad. Sometimes the choices are not very wise that people make, and because the police officers made an unwise choice, we now are left with the consequence that Austin will never be with us again until we meet him in heaven. I believe it would be much better to speak these words to those who are going through the tragedy of losing a loved one: "I wish I had all the answers for you, but I do know a God who cares and who will carry you through your time of sorrow."
- "Time heals all wounds": Time doesn't heal all wounds, although healing takes time. These words would be better said: "You will always miss him, and you will never forget him. I do pray that in time God will heal you from the deep grief you are carrying right now."

Numerous people have reached out to our family with love and compassion. Our friends and family were of great comfort to us. They grieved with us as they shared memories of Austin. His closest friends crawled into my lap and wept. Cards, flowers, and gifts were sent to our home. I could never thank each one of these people enough for their generous giving and outpouring of love. It was truly unbelievable to see such a large number (too many to count) of friends and family we had in the time of desperation and need.

These are some of the things that are very comforting to someone who is mourning:

Very comforting statements:
- "I am praying for you."
- "I am sorry."
- "I admired him or her because…" It brought some joy to us knowing that Austin touched the hearts of many people, not only his family.
- "I don't know what to say; just know I love you." Feeling the support from family and friends is the most important. We knew we were not alone.
- "My thoughts and prayers are with you." We couldn't have made it without the prayers from our dear family and friends. Thank God for them!

Helpful things to do:
- Allow the grieving person to express his or her feelings when he or she is ready.
- Acknowledge their pain. Tell them it is okay to feel that way.
- Talk about the person they have lost. Jack and I longed to hear stories about Austin. In a sense, he still seemed alive to us that way.
- Provide comfort and support to grieving children also—not only parents.
- Communicate your love by saying nothing with a gentle hug.
- Be specific with offers of help and follow up (food,

phone calls, or babysit). Sometimes it may help to bring frozen casserole dishes to warm up later.
- Send flowers or cards to show you haven't forgotten.
- Offer your support: "Tell me what I can do for you."
- Listen with compassion.
- Accept and acknowledge all feelings the person is having.
- Help with funeral arrangements.
- Gather pictures you may have of the person who passed away.
- Stay in their home to take phone calls or receive guests.
- Look after their pets.
- Accompany them on a walk.
- Take them to lunch or a movie when they feel ready.
- Look through photos with them.
- Remember the grieving person for weeks and months after losing their loved one with another card or a phone call to reassure them you have not forgotten. Remembering important dates, such as the anniversary of their death or a birthday is also comforting.

"But those who hope in the Lord will renew their strength. They will soar on wings like eagles; they will run and not grow weary, they will walk and not be faint" (Isaiah 40:31).

# Where are we Now?
## (Concluding Thoughts)

*"Please, God, help him!" My overwhelmed mind seems to give way, immediately flashing back to a series of thoughts from before…*

My mind still gives way at times when I relive those moments in my mind. I immediately break out in a sweat and my heart begins racing one hundred miles per hour—just like that moment when I began screaming and not taking a moment of breath. There was nothing more difficult than finding out our child lost his life. He was gone from our lives for as long as we live.

It was and still is very difficult to live with. We will no longer be able to hug him or hold him. There were no more memories to be made. We will no longer be able to push him in the swing or sit and read him a book. I will never be able to see my husband get down in the floor and wrestle with Austin again. Dalton will no longer be able to play and chase him again. We do not get to hear Austin's sweet voice or laughter within the hallways of our home. Our family misses the simplest things in life as we have to continue living without him here on Earth. We miss seeing him grow older. We wonder how tall he would have been. What would he have become? It is difficult sometimes to see his little friends maturing and growing up. He will always be a little five year old boy in our minds—*forever*.

Many people have asked us how we are handling it now. "How do you go on with your lives?" they ask. We are still grieving in many ways, but we are not letting it keep us from embracing God's love and trying to lift the spirits of those who are suffering. Since the horrible tragedy, we have had several opportunities to visit with other families going through their own devastating situations and their own unimaginable tragedies. It is almost as if we have become "family" because we understand each other's grief. It may not be the exact situation, but it is still grief beyond despair, and we can relate to those emotions. We wrap our arms around each individual within these families. Many times, the tears will be streaming down our faces and we can hardly say a word. I believe that is the primary key, though, to get through the intense heartache—help someone else in *their* need and *their* situation. We open our hearts to them, surround them with as much love and support as possible, and this in turn helps us heal.

Our strength comes from the Lord. Isaiah 41:30 says: "But those who wait on the LORD shall renew their strength; they shall mount up with wings like eagles, they shall run and not be weary, they shall walk and not faint." The Hebrew word for wait in Isaiah 40:31 means *to bind together, look patiently, tarry, wait.* Therefore, we continue to wait for the Lord's return when he takes us all to Heaven and we are able to see Austin once again, run up to him, give him the longest and sweetest hug we have ever had, and spend forever and forever with him. Someday there will be no more tears—no more heartache—and how we look forward to and yearn for that day. Eternity is just around the corner. With every passing second, eternity becomes more of a reality. For now, we bind ourselves together as a family and with others who need to be uplifted in their time of troubles. We look forward as much as possible to the future, instead of looking back to those things that cannot be changed. By doing this, He gives us strength through each and every day. 2 Corinthians 4:18 says, "While we do not look at the things which are seen, but at the things which are not seen. For the things which are seen *are* temporary, but the things which are not seen *are* eternal." The

# Where are We Now?
## (Concluding Thoughts)

family we have now—our house, the pleasures of this life—are all temporary. Trials are all temporary. We are fighting a fight that is only *temporary*.

Rather than temporary things, we need to focus on the eternal. Our family focuses on Heaven and the things in it because life after death is *forever*, something that is never going to end. There will be no more mourning or tears. For, what is unseen is eternal. We are traveling to a home that will not be broken. Praise God, when we leave this world, we will have a crown of glory and be with our Lord *and* our son, Austin, forevermore.

God has His own ways of calming our fears and heartaches as long as we stay focused on Him. In August of this year, two years after Austin's death, I was putting Dalton to bed when he told me the most beautiful story I had heard in a long time:

> "Mama, I saw Austin last night while lying in my bed. He appeared through my ceiling. He said he came because he missed me and wanted to give me a hug and a kiss. It felt so good to see him again. He stayed and played with me in my room for a while. Then I said, 'Austin, I wish we could go out to play, but it's too dark outside right now.' Austin told me, 'That's okay. We can go outside because God turns the night into day.' When Austin opened the front door, it immediately went from night to day, so we played on the swing set. Then we ran and played. It was nice. After that, Austin asked me, 'Do you want to come to heaven with me for a little while?' I said, 'sure,' so Jesus came down from heaven, took my hand, and lifted me up to heaven. You'll never guess what's in heaven! There's a healing tree there... That's what healed Austin! There is orange stuff in it that heals people. Austin called it, 'The Tree of Life.' He took me to a river where a bunch of fish jumped in and out of the water while they swam. There are a ton of angels in heaven, and they sing really nice. It makes God and Jesus smile when they sing. He showed me his huge house that sits on the biggest rock ever. Then, we went and played on a huge swing that went up high in the air, but it didn't scare me because nobody gets scared in heaven. We slid on a slide that went around and around and around.... as long as you wanted to slide, it kept going. After we played in Heaven, I started getting sleepy. So, Jesus and Austin

brought me back and laid me down in my bed. I told Austin, 'I'm sorry. My eyes are starting to go closed. I'm getting sleepy now.' Austin leaned over and gave me a kiss on the cheek and said, 'That's okay, I've got to go back to heaven to be with God and Jesus, but meet me in heaven some day.' I was glad I got to see him again. I love him so much."

By the time he had finished the story, I had tears dripping off my chin, and I was shaking from head to toe. I knew he couldn't make this story up because Jack and I had taught him as much about heaven as we could ... about God, Jesus, the angels, the river, but we had never thought about mentioning the Tree of Life before! Dalton felt so special and loved by Austin that night. Not too long after, he drew a picture of what he saw in heaven that day, and I keep that in my Bible as a constant reminder.... God has always taken care of us and always will take care of us. Thank you, God, for helping us through each and every day.

Many times when life is unbelievably difficult and we cannot bear any more pain or heartache, God gives us something good in our lives. He will never put on us more than we can bear (1 Corinthians 10:13). God cares for us, and He loves us. Whatever your struggle is, if you are going through an unimaginable tragedy, just remember God will carry you through. When things seem so difficult, find the good things and think about them. If you need to, develop a list of all the good things God has done in your life.

You may not understand why you have to go through this trial you are facing right now, but God is in control. I am sure Job did not understand why he continued losing everything in his life, including his entire family. In the book of Daniel, Shadrach, Meshach, and Abednego were taken to a fiery furnace, left to die. I am sure they didn't understand, but as they kept their faith in God, not even the hair on their heads was singed from the fiery furnace. As Paul prayed to God for all he was going through as he sat in jail for doing nothing wrong, he most likely began wondering, *What have I done to deserve this*? But he kept the faith, and he believed that God would help him in the end. God was merciful, and His presence was with

## Where are We Now?
### (Concluding Thoughts)

Paul to the very end, as God will be with you. The Bible is full of testimonies of God's sustaining power in times of trouble or need. I pray as you read this book, whatever your situation is right now, that God will help, encourage you, and strengthen you every day. Somehow He will bring you through the unimaginable. Jesus says, "I am the Lord that healeth thee." And he says:

> For assuredly, I say to you, whoever says to this mountain, 'Be removed and be cast into the sea,' and does not doubt in his heart, but believes that those things he says will be done, he will have whatever he says. Therefore I say to you, whatever things you ask when you pray, believe that you receive them, and you will have them.
> 
> Mark 11:23–24

We hope as a family to accomplish several things in the writing of this book. First and foremost, if you do not know Jesus Christ as your Savior, come to Him today. It is as simple as A, B, C:

A: Ask—ask Jesus to come into your heart.

B: Believe—believe in Jesus Christ and that He died for you.

C: Confess—confess your sins to the Lord and ask Him to remove them from your life.

The Bible says, "If you confess with your mouth the Lord Jesus and believe in your heart that God has raised Him from the dead, you will be saved" (Romans 10:9). As stated in the Amplified Bible, the word "believe" means "to trust in, rely upon, and adhere to." Therefore, when you believe, you trust in Jesus, rely upon Him, and adhere to the Word of God.

The "prayer of salvation" is the most important prayer we'll ever pray. When we're ready to become a Christian, we're ready to have our first real conversation with God. When we pray the prayer of salvation, we're letting God know we believe His Word is true. By the faith He has given us, we choose to believe in Him. The Bible tells us that "without faith it is impossible to please Him, for he who comes to God must believe that he is; and that He is a rewarder of those who "diligently seek Him." (Hebrews 11:6) So, when we pray, asking God for the gift of salvation, we're exercising our free will to acknowledge that we believe in Him. That demonstration of faith pleases God, because we have freely chosen to know Him. When we pray for salvation, we're also admitting that we've sinned. As the Bible says, "For all have sinned, and fall short of the glory of God." (Romans 3:23) Because God could only accept a perfect, sinless sacrifice, and because He knew that we could not possibly accomplish that, He sent His Son to die for us and pay the eternal price, "For God so loved the world that He gave His only begotten Son, that whosoever believes in Him should not perish but have everlasting life." (John 3:16)

> If you believe in your heart all of these things and have not prayed this prayer before, I urge you to make the right choice and pray these words with me right now:
> "Heavenly Father, I recognize now that You are God. I know I have not lived my life the way You have really wanted me to. I ask You to forgive me of my sins. I believe Jesus is Your Son, that He was born and lived on earth. He took the sins of man and died on the cross for all mankind. I believe three days later He arose from the grave alive and ascended into heaven so the Holy Spirit could come and give me comfort. Jesus, please come into my heart. I know now that my name is written down in the Lamb's Book of Life, and I am ready to live for You. I am willing to take direction from You. Please guide me in my life beginning this very day—this very moment of my life. I love You, God, and I love You, Jesus, because You first loved me. Amen."

If you have prayed this prayer from your heart, you are now in the family of God! God's Holy Spirit will help you now. If you will spend time with God on a daily basis, He will lead and guide you. Any person can be saved. All you have to do is believe. Revelation 3:20 says, "Behold, I stand at the door and knock. If anyone hears My voice and opens the door, I will come in to him and dine with him and he with Me."

Jesus wants us all to hear his voice and open the door of our hearts to him. If we do, this verse says he will dine with us, meaning he will provide for the needs of your heart.

# Where are We Now?
## (Concluding Thoughts)

To this date eighty-eight people have testified and contacted us to say that they came to know the Lord through the testimony of Austin. Second, if you have been saved through this testimony, let us know, as we want to know how many stars may be in Austin's crown before we meet him in heaven. Our Web site is www.austinhaley.com. This gives us much comfort. Third, if you are facing the unimaginable tragedy, whatever it may be, I am praying for you today.

I want you to receive this prayer:

Dear Lord,

I am asking that You will pour out the oil of healing onto this broken heart today. Lord, You know their situation, and You know what unimaginable circumstance they are going through right now. I pray that You would give them comfort and give them peace that passes all understanding. Many times, we do not understand why we have to go through life's struggles, but, Lord, supply their need, as they are allowing You to take control of their life. Lord, help them to praise You while on the mountain when everything is fine in their lives and nothing is going wrong, and also help them to turn their focus to You even in the valley—in the darkest and lowest part of their life. Give them strength, dear Lord, to endure another minute, another hour, another day. I pray You would touch them right now as they are sitting and reading this book. Help them to feel Your spirit, Lord. Help them to feel Your strength and power come directly into their lives. Thank You, Lord, for all that You do. Amen.

I am going to ask God to pour the oil of healing onto your soul and bring about a true healing in your life. My prayer is that God will lift you up.

# When Adversity Comes Against You

## and the Keys to Overcome It

### By Jack Haley

Grief comes in many forms, and anger is one of them. As the adversity that we faced continued, I became very angry. I could not help it. Losing my five-year-old son was very difficult to endure and still is, and I needed God's help. God had given me a family. I felt it was my duty to take care of them. It was difficult seeing Austin pass from my life. Our wonderful family would never be the same again. In Easton's 1897 Bible Dictionary, the definition of a husband is referred to as "house band." I felt God had placed me on this earth to "band" my house together and take care of each one of them. It continues to state the definition as "connecting and keeping together the whole family." To endure the thought of not having the entire family together anymore was more than I could handle at times. Our family would never be complete again—we would always be missing one child. I needed God's help to endure such heartache.

Losing Austin was not the first time I have had to endure loss. My own mother went through her own unthinkable tragedy, losing a son (my brother, Daniel Haley) and her husband (my father, Floyd Haley) in May of 1975; I recall that I was almost five years old. A semi tractor and trailer lost control on a bridge. My dad was driving a truck with a trailer hauling a John Deere tractor for a customer. The semi jackknifed, and there was no place for my dad to get out of the situation. My brother was killed instantly, while my dad only lived for a short while after the accident. My mother's life was turned upside down. She was a housewife who had just lost the love of her life. She did not know how to drive, and she also had to find a job to support her children. Life was not easy for her. Since the accident, our family, among brothers and sisters, has grown, and there are many grandchildren and great-grandchildren, and we have all come a long way since then.

My mother is the reason for our family of siblings being close knit and together today. She alone continued on with her faith, strength, and courage to continue raising her children. After the tragedy of losing her husband and son, she still had six children at home to care and provide for. Beating cancer along the way in the early 80's, she stuck with the job and did not say no. Since she never remarried, I know it was not easy. She had to do it all alone.

I do not believe that I ever mourned the death of my father or brother until I lost my son. I grew up without a father, so I did not know what having a father was supposed to feel like. Losing Austin when he was five years old and my being five years old when I lost my dad and brother was too much of a link to not have an effect on me. When I first saw Austin lying in the back of Grandpa's Polaris after his fatal injury, I knew his life was over. I yelled, repeating, "What happened, Jack?" and I dropped to my knees immediately. I could not help it, my knees buckled and I absolutely could not get up. I was robbed of so much, of getting to see him grow into a teenager and then to manhood. I thought to myself, *what have I done to deserve so much pain*? How was I supposed to endure the days, months, and years without Austin? The only way to endure would be to call on God to carry me and my family through these times.

It seemed as though all of the odds were against us when the accident took place. Losing our son had put us in a position that was incomprehensible, too. Never would I have imagined how closely our town, state, and nation were watching as the days unfolded after the accident. Try and put yourself in my position for a moment and imagine that the faces of you, your wife, and your child have just been pasted all over the media, Internet, and papers for the world to see. Now imagine that it is because a police officer, sworn to uphold the law, just killed your child out of negligence; now the local television stations want to know how you feel about it. What are you going to say? How are you going to present yourself? What are you going to do? Do you respond? Do you go into your house and hide? Or do you stand up for what you know is right? Do we stand up and say what happened to us was wrong?

As the head of my family, I was faced with all of these questions. I was reminded of a verse my mother quoted to me from the Bible, saying, "Now when they bring you to the synagogues and magistrates and authorities, do not worry about how or what you should answer or what you should say. For the Holy Spirit will teach you in that very hour what you ought to say" (Luke 12:11–12).

As a family we decided that we must stand up and fight for what was right. I began to write a letter to the Cleveland County District Attorney. I stated in my letter what my thoughts were on the incident and requested to meet with him to talk about what happened and what our course of action could be. Upon meeting with the District Attorney, our initial impressions were not good. We had hoped he would be on the same page as we were, considering the officers had broken the law. His first suggestions would only give the officers probation. Since the police officers had made such a poor decision, we were not satisfied with probation alone. The fact that the officers chose to use a weapon of deadly force inside city limits in a non-emergency situation was a violation of the local law, which reads that for a weapon of deadly force to be used inside city limits, there must be a person or public in danger. No person was in danger, so there was no reason to shoot. Therefore, we were hoping the district attorney would have been sympathetic to our cause. We wanted to see a short jail sentence for both of the officers, something that would say to all police and public alike, "If you do this kind of thing and someone dies because of it, you will see jail time."

The district attorney did not agree with our suggestion. We know that he and the assistant DA were attempting to protect the officers from any real kind of justice. The district attorney and his assistant came up with a sweetheart of a deal for the officers, and they took it. Behind our backs, the offer was made to them. We did not have an opportunity to stop it. So we contacted the only advocates we had—the media.

When we found out that a bargain had been reached, we went straight to the news and told them what deal was made. We knew there was some kind of deal struck because the officers waived their rights to a jury trial. We knew we could get some kind of results; maybe not all of what we wanted, but some. Our decision to go to the media enraged the assistant DA, and he had actually decided to make a phone call and tell me about it. I do not recall the full context of the conversation, but some of his final words were very hurtful to me, implying that I was only doing all of this to bring my son back. His call and the words we exchanged only confirmed the fact that we were not adequately represented by the officials elected to do so.

When it was all said and done, we still did not get what we wanted. Even before the judge had lowered his gavel and the former officers were being counseled by their attorneys, we tried to counsel with ours, the assistant DA. We asked him, "If these officers do not accept the deal and there has to be a trial, are you and the district attorney going to fight for us?" He just simply said no, and the DA would most likely get a special prosecutor if that were the case. At that moment in time, even the district attorney's office was not on our side. All I could think was that the law was broke and my son died because of it, and you will not help us? The judge, after hearing two hours of what he said was the most compelling testimony from any case he had ever heard, gave the former officers several months of community service along with probation.

That decision caused us disappointment. They were shown bias by the court, and by the Cleveland County DA's Office. However, I will be able to live with myself for not cowering in the face of great adversity. I can live with myself for the fact that I at least let the world know what these officers did was wrong. It is all part of taking a stand for what you believe in.

"The steps of a good man are ordered by the Lord" (Psalm 37:23).

Thankfully, I have God, and he directs our steps through the highs and lows of life. This is a verse to live by when you think you are drifting off the journey. Remember, as long as you have submitted your life to God and are willing to accept his direction, your steps are ordered and directed by him. Even when it seems it is taking a very long time for the answer to come or destination to become evident, your steps will lead you to the place where God planned for them to be. I pray God will direct you in your journey.

We appreciated the judge for giving our whole family an opportunity to speak in the courtroom and tell the former police officers our feelings. About twelve family members were granted as much time as needed to share their own testimony of grief. Sure, we were all in tears. We were all hurt and angry at the same time. When it came to the end of the case and the judge lowered his gavel, we were disappointed in the fact that not even one day of jail time was given for the police to sit and dwell on their mistake for a while. However, he did increase the sentence to some community service along with the probation. They were both charged with the felony of second degree manslaughter.

We know that what the police officers did was a mistake, but it was a fatal one, caused by breaking the law. They did need some kind of consequence. Someday those officers will have to face God, with Him knowing their heart's intent, and He will judge them as He wills. Hebrews 4:13 says, "And there is no creature hidden from His sight, but all things are naked and open to the eyes of Him to whom we must give account."

We do not know the hearts of the former officers. We can't imagine any reasonable thinking person to make such a hasty decision, but we hope that their hearts have been softened as a result of the accident. We hope that they have now or someday will decide to become closer to God and will get to go to heaven. Otherwise, there is only the judgment of God left for what they did. Considering the circumstances of the accident and their actions when they were officers, considering the laughing and joking around before the shots, it was arrogance that caused them to think that they could somehow kill the snake with a single bullet. The Bible says in Mark 7:21–23, "For from within, out of the heart of men, proceed evil thoughts, adulteries, fornications, murders, thefts, covetousness, wickedness, deceit, lewdness, an evil eye, blasphemy, pride, foolishness. All these evil things come from within and defile a man."

And Proverbs 16:18 says, "Pride goes before destruction, and a haughty spirit before a fall."

We still had to live our lives knowing our son's death was at the hands of two officers who were attempting to kill a snake with a single bullet without a backdrop. And for what—target practice? It is very difficult to live with. We grieve constantly over the loss of our son. We miss him tremendously.

As much as I want to be an overcomer of the tragedy I have gone through, I want you to be an overcomer of yours. But you have to be willing. There are many ways a tragedy can take place in your life, though I pray that none do. There are many people who believe their one unthinkable tragedy is when the IRS audited their tax return. A quick search on the Internet will reveal many examples of how a tragedy can take place. Some involve cancer or diseases, breaking an arm or a leg, a house burning down with all of their belongings. There is the resulting loss of a family member due to drunken driving and so on. There are so many ways a tragedy can form. If you have gone through a tragedy, never discount or degrade what anyone has gone through; try to have a servant's heart.

My hopes and prayers are that no one will ever have to experience what my wife and I have gone through with the loss of a family member, but once you have gone through the unexpected death of a child or someone close to you, you are scarred for life. Honestly, no one knows what you are going through except those who are in that small family of the unfortunate and who have gone through that same loss.

What it means for me to be an overcomer is that I have done all I can do to be at that place before the tragedy. It means being the best father I can be to my children. It means continuing to be a provider and husband to my wife. It means never forsaking what we all have together. It means carrying on your life while serving God and striving to somehow find a happiness that can sustain you. There is a legacy to be lost if that circle is broken. Use your testimony as the bible says. If a person will stand his or her ground and discover that there is still a life to be lived, overcoming your tragedy will someday happen. Never forget what you have gone through, so that you can be of service to others. The following verses prove that there is a way to overcome great problems.

> And they overcame him by the blood of the Lamb and by the word of their testimony, and they did not love their lives to the death.
>
> Revelation 12:11

The meaning of this verse comes to light through your own witness to others. A testimony is commonly referred to as an account of evidence given under oath by a witness. Just as this book and all of its information is an account or witness of what my family has gone through in the past years, your witness, your testimony, can be one in which you have withstood a test, a trial, or tragedy, just as Job, through all of his tribulation, still had a testimony that he had faith in God and all things that he lost were restored to him even greater than what he had before.

> Yet in all these things we are more than conquerors through Him who loved us.
>
> Romans 8:37

By being a conqueror, you have withstood your tragedy and not let the worldly views and consequences overtake you and make you withdraw into a person without hope. If you remember that God does love you and that he gives you grace daily, you will be a conqueror.

> Who is he who overcomes the world, but he who believes that Jesus is the Son of God?
>
> 1 John 5:5

This is a question asked of any person. If you believe in Jesus and that he is the Son of God, then you shall be an overcomer of the world. That is the hope that we should have: to remember that there will be full restoration for those who believe in Christ. The Apostle Paul said in 2 Timothy 4:7–8, "I have fought the good fight, I have finished the race, I have kept the faith. Finally, there is laid up for me the crown of righteousness, which the Lord, the righteous Judge, will give to me on that Day, and not to me only but also to all who have loved His appearing."

My family and I are hopeful that when the day comes we will get to see our Savior, the one who holds our child in his protective arms; to get to see the one who led us out of the darkened days. It is through Jesus alone that we can live today and have hope to overcome what tomorrow has in store.

It is especially important for husbands and wives to stay together after a tragedy such as this, no matter how hard it may become. I could never imagine for one moment leaving behind a relationship that created the little boy that I loved so much in the first place. [2] A survey was taken documenting the number of parents who have gone through the death of a child; this information includes deaths at birth and miscarriages conducted by Directions Research Inc. for Compassionate Friends Inc. The research showed there were nearly 980,000 deaths in the year 1996. In the years 1999 and 2006, four hundred persons related to the deaths in 1996 were a part of the survey. Of these four hundred, 306 persons were married at the time of their loss, 16 percent, of those had divorced. Of the original 980,000 deaths that happened, nearly two million lives were affected by those deaths, when applying the same percentages to those two million, the possibility that over three hundred thousand lives were also affected by divorce, is evident. That is a shocking number. Of those surveyed, 40 percent actually admit their marriages were affected by the death of their loved one, a major reason for their divorce.

What I do not understand is, *why?* You may find yourself wanting to get away from the pain and the pressure of what you are going through; you may think that you are doing yourself a favor in the end. But in the end, what has been gained? The lives that needed your guidance and direction, your love and devotion, would simply be broken again. Stay together and build a life out of the tragedy; trust in God, and don't blame Him for actions that take place on this earth. He sent his Son, Jesus Christ, who said, "I have come that they may have life, and that they have it more abundantly" (John 10:10).

I can honestly say that not every day I live is a happy day primarily because of our tragedy, but if you are allowing God and His Son to help you along the way, there will be some happy days to remember.

Conversely, the survey mentioned earlier also includes information about how those parents received support. Not surprising to me was how 80 percent of those parents' support came from friends and family. Friends and family can support those family members who are going through a tragedy by just being there for that loved one; just holding a hand and putting an arm on the shoulder and saying, "I am here for you."

> "I am here for you."

That went a long way with Renee and me. Just knowing that someone was there for us was important. It was very important to me to have my older brothers and sisters nearby to talk to and just be there for support. A person does not need to say much to encourage. The saying is true that actions speak louder than words. It is best to leave your words few so that a word is not taken wrong from you. Words said in haste do not always contain the best wisdom for a person going through a tragedy. Just taking the time to spend with that person or occupying his or her time with a movie or helping with chores around the house is helpful. One thing that helped me tremendously was when my wife's younger brothers helped me out by mowing my lawn, which is no easy task. I was very thankful for that.

There are going to be those people who think you should blame God for your tragedy. We did not blame God. One reason we did not came from the fact that we have been serving Him for a number of years, and with time comes knowledge and faith. We know the God we serve does not cause bad things to happen to His people. But God will use a tragedy to bring other people closer to Him. Unexpected tragedies have a way of getting the attention of those that hear of them, including Christians and non-Christians alike. One verse as evidence comes from 2 Samuel 14:14, and it says, "For we will surely die and become like water spilled on the ground, which cannot be gathered up again. Yet God does not take away a life; but he devises means, so that his banished ones are not expelled from him."

This means that God will use the tragedy to bring another person who was running from Him closer to Him. The Bible says we are promised to die once and then to be judged. Hebrews 9:27 says, "And as it is appointed for men to die once, but after this the judgment."

This is simply just a fact. All of us are going to die at one time or another, although life is not ours to take; it is not our place to judge when it will take place. Therefore, it is of utmost importance to know where you stand with God before death. So that once you do stand in front of God, who is the judge, you know that your sins are covered by Christ who died for your sins. Please give your life to Christ.

If you are going through a trial, a tragedy, or whatever it may be, there is certainly help from God. God's Word is amazing in that it does not return void, and it has been a comfort to me during our tragedy and now. It gives me assurance to know that someday I will get to see my son again. Austin's favorite verse in the Bible was from

Jeremiah 17:7: "But blessed is the man who trusts in the Lord, whose confidence is in him."

It is a verse that became the theme for everything in our lives after the accident. One way this verse has helped is in my need for fatherly control and protection. I was the type of father who thought every aspect of my child's well-being was covered. Little did I know of the surprise and finality that bullet would have. I had spent four years in the military (United States Air Force), which gave me a lifetime perspective of discipline, leadership, and protection. I was an aircraft crew chief in charge of the safety of a fighter aircraft and the well-being of the crew that flew it. I have been involved in the maintenance and restoration of aircraft for twenty years now, and for eight of those years I have been an aircraft inspector at Tinker Air Force Base, where I work as a civilian. So with that in mind, discipline, leadership, and protection come into play many times a day. I have always felt that with my experiences from a short but successful military career, with enough thought, preparation, planning, and action, I could solve any problem.

I have always prided myself with being able to fix most things. Even my wife cannot believe me at times when I say I can fix something and then do it. I was always protective of Austin from early on. I would make sure his hand was held by either me or Mama while crossing the street; how we didn't leave his side when we were in a small swimming pool outside, or how we made sure he had a life jacket on at the lake. My children's protection has always been my highest priority. However, I could not protect Austin from a bullet. When that problem came my way, I did not know what to do. When I first saw his injury, I knew there was no way I could help him. The injury was final—I knew it. However, I still prayed over him many times after I saw him, I guess I was trying to bring him back to me. In that moment, the only tool I could use was the power of prayer.

At the hospital, when we saw him for the first time after the ambulance took him, we could hardly believe that our wonderful boy was gone from his body. We dropped to our knees at his bedside and praised God for the wonderful, faithful little boy He had provided us with. That was all we could think about: how faithful Austin was to God; how Austin had taught us so many things about life; how important God was to him. It is so important to have hope in the Lord, beyond this world.

Trusting in the Lord gave me the strength to conquer another fear. Ever since getting married and having our children, my fear of dying and leaving my family behind was my greatest fear. Since I had lost my father at such a young age, I feared leaving my wife and children behind at their young ages. When I lost my dad I was almost five years old, and I know the effects not having a father can have on a child. I have lived it my entire life, and I did not want that for my own children. But yet, in the back of my mind, I feared somehow that it would be me. I no longer have that fear. Placed in the hands of God, my fears were released. I welcome the day when I get to meet my Savior and get to see family I have longed for; not that I want that day to get here any faster; there are many things in this life that we have yet to accomplish. Hebrews 12:1–2 best describe my thoughts on this issue:

> Therefore we also, since we are surrounded by so great a cloud of witnesses, let us lay aside every weight, and the sin which so easily ensnares us, and let us run with endurance the race that is set before us, looking unto Jesus, the author and finisher of our faith, who for the joy that was set before him endured the cross, despising the shame, and has sat down at the right hand of the throne of God.

I long to see all of those I have lost, and all of those who have gone on before me. I can only imagine what it will be like on that reunion day.

It is good to continue serving God during a tragedy by volunteering and reaching out to others. Volunteer your services for a church, teach Sunday school, or make yourself available to be used in ways where there is a need. Volunteer in your community also. Your service does not necessarily have to be for a church; however, it is good to do so. God recognizes service and labors given in many ways, and when given from the heart, it can be healing enough to get you through many days of your tragedy. Also, it is helpful when you hear of other people who have withstood their own storms in their life to go to them and offer ways you can help. Share your tragedy and let them know they are not alone and that there is a comforter in the form of the Savior, who is Jesus Christ. The Bible says in 2 Corinthians 1:1–7:

> Blessed be the God and Father of our Lord Jesus Christ, the Father of mercies and God of all comfort, who comforts us in all our tribulation that we may be able to comfort those who are in any trouble, with the comfort with which we ourselves are comforted by God. For as the sufferings of Christ abound in us, so our consolation also abounds through Christ. Now if we are afflicted, it is for your consolation and salvation, which is effective for enduring the same sufferings which we also suffer. Or if we are comforted, it is for your consolation and salvation. And our hope for you is steadfast, because we know that as you are partakers of the sufferings, so also you will partake of the consolation.

This speaks volumes alone without having to explain. However, the Apostle Paul was so sure when he wrote this, through the inspiration of the Holy Spirit; he knew we would be comforted by Christ's sufferings; that we, through the witness of even Paul's struggles, would come to know Christ so that even though we go through tribulation and struggles, we would partake in the consolation that comes through salvation. We know many people hurt with us and for us because of our tragedy. We were also consoled because of the knowledge of so many who were saved because of the tragedy. Eighty-eight people we know of have communicated that they turned their lives over to Christ. New friendships were born out of that knowledge. We are so thankful for those friendships. There are also many we pray for who still have not yet come to the knowledge of Christ but are still touched by the death of Austin in ways that soften their hearts, and we pray that someday they are consoled in the same manner we are.

If anything sticks in you mind from this chapter, let it be "stand up for what you believe in." Don't let the world decide what you will do. If you have God on your side and have asked Jesus into your heart, then the Holy Spirit will guide you and help you make more conscious decisions. If you decide that you will not stand, then you will always wonder what could have been. So take your chance.

# A Father's Memories

## Written by Jack Haley

When Austin was born I said to myself, "I account him as a miracle." Austin was, from the start, the type of boy that any father would have been proud of to carry on the family name. He was my boy—Austin Gabriel Haley. His mother gave him his first name, and I gave him his middle name. From the time that he started showing little-boy tendencies, I could see myself in him. When he would talk, when he would run, and when he would play, he looked and acted so much like me when I was a child. He made me want to take an active role in being a father, and I always will try to take an active role in parenting my children by being a good example to them. I will always make sure that they learn what they need to learn about life and how to carry themselves. I will always make sure that they know they are loved by their father, by telling them so. I will always miss my son, and I will never forget his example to me—how he lived and how he loved and how he made sure that he told me so. It is a sign of strength, not weakness, for a man to express his love for his wife and children.

"This is my son, Austin, in whom I am well pleased." This is

> "This is my son, Austin, in whom I am well pleased."

what I said to his grandpa, the day he was born. I handed Austin to him as I said those words to Renee's father, Jack, knowing that there would be a special relationship between Austin and him. I did not get to say those words to my own father. But it was an honor to hand my son to his only living grandpa, Jack Tracy, as Austin would be Jack's first grandson. Austin loved his grandpa very much. But Austin loved his mama and daddy too. "He loved hanging out with his daddy, me; and when Dalton came along, well, then there were three."

> "He loved hanging out with his daddy, me; and when Dalton came along, well, then there were three."

I would have done anything for that boy. I gave him pretty much everything he ever asked for because he showed us how much he loved us. But the little things meant the most to Austin. He wanted to hear that you loved him, too. I would sometimes take my boys out to the Saturday swap meet in Oklahoma City and have the greatest time. They would find the best toys out there. Austin was very picky; he wanted the biggest bang for the buck. He knew what he wanted when he saw it. He would pick up a toy and look at it and ask me what I thought. I'd tell him, "Whatever you think you want, son; it's your choice." Sometimes we came out of there with a dozen toys, and then sometimes one. And that one would mean so much to him.

It meant so much to me for Austin to know what little thing about him I treasured. For example, he could run. He could run like no other child I had ever seen. I used to go jog at the track at the high school where we lived, and his mama would walk him around with Dalton. Austin would take off running behind me, and he, at three years old, could run a full lap around the track without stopping.

> Oh, how I lived through that boy!

That pleased me so much to see that in him. Oh, how I lived through that boy!

I was a track runner in school from junior high up through high school, but I stopped when I went into the military. From time to time I have tried to get back into the shape I once was, but to no avail. So it pleased me to see that my son could carry himself so willingly and ready to go. Sometimes when I would see him run from inside the house, he would run like the wind, and if he saw me peeking out at him, he would somehow slow down as if I was not supposed see how fast he really was. I guess he was humble.

He was not humble with girls. He loved girls, and oh, how they loved him. He had "girlfriends" like crazy—at school, at daycare, everywhere he went, even at the mall. If a girl his age spotted him and he spotted her, he wanted to know who she was and what her name was.

It's hard now to fathom that all I have are memories of him to keep. Sure, I have some of his toys, some of his papers that show his writing, pictures and videos of him, but I know that things will never be the same again. There will always be an empty place at the dinner table, a seat that should have been filled by him for the trip to the swap meet, and a lost opportunity for Austin to be in his room playing with his little brothers.

I counted on Austin, and I know that his mother and Dalton did too. As we were watching our son Austin grow, he was teaching, guiding and protecting his little brother, Dalton, along the way. Dalton misses his big brother in a much needed way. Dalton was meant to have a big brother and we as his parents have been shown in the few years since Austin's death, that Dalton needs very special attention to fill that void. Now that Dalton is a big brother to Gabriel, he has taken on that roll to fill some very big shoes that Austin left for him.

A comforting memory I will always have is when I received an almost immediate answer to my prayers. Renee and I had returned to the funeral home to finish arrangements for the funeral and to view Austin for the first time since the hospital. We were praying and crying over him for what seemed like hours. I distinctly remember leaning over him and talking to him, hoping that I would somehow hear from heaven. I know that I heard Austin's voice when I heard him say, "Daddy," in a laughing voice, "I'm not in there; I am up here." I immediately said out loud to him, "Austin, go to God and ask him to send us a message from you." I was so desperate I was willing to say or do anything to hear from God or Austin. A few hours later, we decided to leave and go back to visit with Renee's mother and father and all the other family members. We had sat down to eat something when Renee felt cold and decided to get up and get a blanket from her mother's linen closet. When she reached inside the closet, she grabbed the first blanket she could get her hands on. She unfolded the blanket and found it had writing on it. She found a blanket that was given to her daddy some years ago for Father's Day. It had Austin's favorite verse on it, Jeremiah 17:7. She eagerly came into the room where we all were, showing everybody what it said. I noticed that she was still holding it folded so that only the verse showed, and I wanted to see what else the blanket said on it. The top part of the blanket showed a message to fathers, and the bottom portion had Austin's favorite verse written on it. When Renee had it folded, only the verse was seen. So I asked her to unfold it and hold up the entire blanket for everyone to see. I could not believe what it said. I knew in my heart that it was a message to me directly from Austin. I believed, without a doubt, that he had gone to his heavenly Father, God, and had been granted permission to send me, his earthly father, this special gift. I almost felt Austin speaking into my soul that day. A poem by T. Tilley said:

### Dad
My Dad is strong in character.
When times may test his faith, he stays
Steadfast and sturdy, trusting in God's grace.

My dad is wise and caring,
Strong but gentle, too; and there's
Nothing like God's blessing of an earthly father, you.

Dreams I have while sleeping have also been a special comfort to me. I often dwell on them because they have helped me along this journey. One dream in particular that is a blessing to me day after day is when I saw a horse and a rider from a great distance. The rider was coming toward me, and I was in a large, open, fielded area like a large valley because we were surrounded by what seemed to be small hills. As the rider came closer, I began to see it was Austin. He was still a little five-year-old boy, but he had a serious look on his face. As he got closer to me, he stopped the horse and turned it sideways as if to show me something. He was in full control of this horse. The horse was reddish brown, large, and powerful. I was so amazed. When Austin turned the horse sideways, he made the horse rise on his hind legs, and Austin revealed a large sword. He was wielding this sword as if he knew what he was doing. He then returned the horse to all fours and rode away. It was an amazing, glorious, and powerful dream to me. I know the dream caused me to feel reassured of Austin's place in heaven. He is in the Lord's Army. Of the many dreams I have had about Austin, I can say that not even one has been a nightmare, replaying the events of his death, and I thank God for that.

# Grandparents' Thoughts and Memories of Austin

## Nanny's Thoughts

Written by paternal grandmother, Bettie Haley:

I'll never forget the day Austin was born—Jack's first son. I held that little boy in my arms, and as I looked at him, he looked at me. His eyes met mine as if he really saw me. I knew then there was something special about him.

As Austin grew, we all could see he had a special gift. By the time he was three years old, he showed a concern and compassion for people. If he knew someone was sad, he was sorry. If they were sick, he would lay his tiny hands on them and ask Jesus to heal them, and he had a perfect faith that they would be healed.

I loved going out to eat with Jack, Renee, and Austin because Austin would sing. He had the sweetest voice, and he put feeling into a song as if he really knew the meaning of the words. It was a joy to hear him.

It's hard for me to talk about Austin. I cherish all my grandchildren, but Austin was my soul mate, my kindred spirit. He was such a happy little boy. One day they came to visit, and I heard him say, "Oh boy, we're at Nanny's, and we can do anything we want!" That just thrilled my soul because I wanted him to enjoy coming to

Nanny's house. I am blessed that all the children still come to play, but it isn't the same. They miss him. He was a gentle leader, and they were drawn to him. They felt his love, his kindness. He was only five years old, but he cared about them and prayed for them with a faith far beyond his years. I am so glad I am getting older. I won't have to wait so long to see him. I feel his love. It gets me through the long and lonely days.

One of my most cherished memories was when I was sitting on a bench in my garden. I felt this little hand slip into mine. He sat beside me for a minute, and we listened to the wind chimes. Then he said in that sweet, clear voice, "I love you, Nanny. I love you, and I love your flowers." Then we hugged each other, and he ran off to play. I felt as if I was touched by an angel.

I could write a thousand thoughts and a thousand memories. But it hurts too much. When he passed away, it didn't just break my heart. It broke my soul. I am waiting for when God calls me. I know what Austin will say: "Welcome home, Nanny. I love you." That will be heaven for me.

—Bettie Haley
Austin's paternal grandmother

## Grandma's Thoughts

Written by maternal grandmother, Cheryl Tracy:

Little Austin, oh, how I miss you; I remember the very moment you were born into this world on October 24, 2001. The very first time I held you in my arms brought Grandma so much joy. You were such a beautiful little miracle of God with dark hair, dark eyes, and so perfect. There were so many family members there at the hospital that we could hardly get into the room, but we all gathered around as your mama and daddy held you with such pride and joy as we sang the song "Jesus Loves Me." We always have lived next door to you, so we had the opportunity to watch you grow during the five years you were with us. My heart melted when I heard you say for the first time, "I love you, Grandma," and I would repeat the words back: "I love you, Austin."

I remember when you got to visit our church, Heavenbound PCG in Norman, Oklahoma. I can still hear your sweet little voice (at the age of three with a surprisingly large vocabulary) when you sat beside me in the fellowship hall as we were eating a church dinner. I will never forget the treasured moment when you looked up (seeing a cross hanging on the wall) and said, "Grandma, there's a cross."

I said, "Yes, baby, it is a cross."

You looked at me with your big, brown eyes and said, "Grandma, put your hand on your heart like this" as you placed your little hand on your own little heart. So Grandma did as you suggested, and I placed my hand upon my heart. Then, to my amazement, with a little louder voice you began to preach like a little preacher: "Jesus lives right there in your heart, and Jesus died for our sins; He shed his blood for us, and He died so we can be saved." Silence began to fill the room, as people were trying to hear this little three-year-old boy tell me about Jesus. Especially now, I treasure that moment very much. Also, Grandma was so proud of you when we could visit your church at Noble Assembly of God and how you would say your memory verse without even missing a word. You were a very special little boy.

I remember all the many good times when Grandma had the opportunity to go shopping with you at the mall. Sometimes I would buy you a little toy, give you quarters to ride a few rides, or simply give you a quarter to let you get gum out of the machine. It didn't matter how big or small it was, your little eyes would light up with happiness as you said, "Thank you, Grandma" and would give me a big hug. Everywhere we went, you always wanted to have a Bible in your hand, even while we were at the mall. You were always letting your little light shine for the Lord.

I remember those times you were with us at Golden Corral restaurant in Norman, Oklahoma, when many of our family members would meet there for a Sunday dinner after church. While we were all sitting around the table, you would tell us the stories you learned while in your Sunday-school class, taught by wonderful teachers, Don and Sandra Colwell. We especially remember you telling us about a Bible story of Balaam and the donkey. It was as though you were doing your best to tell the story just like your teacher told it, which really made us all laugh when you began telling us with very expressive words and actions how God caused the donkey to talk to Balaam.

I remember how I would run and play with you as we would play a little game that you made up. You would hold a little wand in your hand and chase Grandma. When you got close to Grandma, you would point the wand toward me, and I would freeze and stand still. Then I would take the wand in my hand and we would play the same game in reverse order. For some reason, I just couldn't keep up with you, as you always would outrun Grandma.

I remember so many family gatherings when I would hear your laughter while playing with your little cousins. I also recall the five birthday parties when you blew out your candles as your little face lit up with such joy. I remind myself of the times I watched you anxiously open your Christmas gifts from under the Christmas tree.

Little Austin, my precious grandson, oh, how I miss you. I thank God for the treasured memories, which are such a comfort to Grandma. Almost every day I pick up your picture from my dresser, give you a kiss on the cheek, tell you how much I miss you, and assure you that Grandma will see you again, which somehow at that moment brings me closer to you. I look so forward to the day when we will all be reunited in heaven. I long to see your little face, to hold you in my arms, and hear your little voice say, "I love you, Grandma" and I say the words to you, "I love you, Austin."

—Tribute to Austin Gabriel Haley
Love, Grandma Cheryl Tracy

Grandparents' Thoughts
and Memories of Austin

# A Tribute to Austin Haley

Written by maternal grandfather, Jack Tracy I:

It is hard to know where to start to write a tribute to Austin. From the time he was born, he was special. He was my first grandson, and I thought he was so handsome. But he had an inner beauty that was more important as he developed and grew older. He was a remarkable young man.

I will always remember how he ran at full blast everywhere he went. He was so full of energy. He loved his little brother and nurtured and hovered over him. He loved his mother and father, grandparents, and friends.

One of the greatest legacies is his love of God. He expressed his love of God almost every day. He carried his Bibles, quoted Bible verses, and prayed for his family, including me. He was destined to be a preacher, teacher, prophet, or evangelist. He was my little man. I loved him with all my heart. One of his last prayers was for my healing. His desire was that others would come to know his Jesus. It seemed as though he was always thinking of others.

I think of our last few minutes together. He wanted to go fishing at our pond. It was one of the joys of life we liked to share. We went to the pond to feed the fish and catch one. Little did we know that he only had minutes to live. As tragic as his death was, I am glad I was with him to the very end and held him in his death as I clutched him and struggled carrying him up the hill to the four-wheeler. I prayed so desperately that there could be some miracle to save his life, but it was not so. I will cherish the memories of the fish we caught, our memories together, and the love we shared for life.

I know he is waiting for me at heaven's gates. I long to see him, to hold him, and to be able to express my love to him again. I want to kiss him again and enjoy spending time with him in a whole, healed body. Yes, heaven will be wonderful. I expect that the river of life will have fish for us to catch. I will see him again. In my dreams I see him running to meet me just as he did in life.

In this book, I pray that others will come to know healing and wholeness, love, and compassion. We all want to strike the devil a blow and help dear people down life's path. Austin's life and even his death will not be in vain. He was quite a little man. May God bless him today!

—By Grandpa: Jack Tracy, Sr.

## Remembering My Precious Little Great-Grandson, Austin Haley

Written by maternal great-grandmother, Dixie Gillum:

It brought us such joy when we received the call on October 24, 2001, from Jack, Austin's daddy. He was taking Renee to the hospital because it was time for Austin to be born. The excitement was in the air as both sides of the family stood in the hallway, waiting to hear that first little cry from Jack and Renee's firstborn son. How happy we all were; we stood around the bed when the nurse let us in and sang "Jesus Loves Me," as we do with all the babies born in our family. It was a precious and sacred moment as Jack Haley handed Jack Tracy little Austin and said, "This is my son in whom I am well pleased." It brought tears to everyone there. As I held Austin, I felt such warmth come over me; I knew he was special and God had His hand upon him.

What a special little boy he became as he got older—the joy he brought to all our family. Austin loved to fish with his grandpa, Jack, and great-grandpa, Jim. His great-grandpa would bait his hook and play with him often. Austin would get excited when he caught a fish. When we had our family dinners, he loved playing with his cousins so much. I enjoyed sitting and listening to them all laugh and play games. All of the children were close to one another. Words cannot express how blessed we all were because of Austin. It was plain to see how God had His hand upon him. No matter where we went, he always talked about Jesus. At two and three years of age, he wanted to carry his Bible, at times one in each hand. Austin once saw a one-way sign on the side of the road while on the way to the mall. He said, "Mama, that sign reminds me of the song 'One Way, Jesus!'" He had the sweetest little voice yet spoke with such depth and wisdom.

Austin's little brother, Dalton, who was two at the time, would get Austin's attention sometimes by lovingly hitting Austin so he would play with him. One time Dalton hit a little too hard, not realizing how hard he was hitting since he was so young. Austin was always so kind to his little brother, and this time he said, "Little brother, don't hit too hard. Bubba loves you." Austin always loved and helped his little brother. He even helped potty train Dalton by playing with him and bragging on him every day.

The short five years we were blessed to have him on this earth will never be forgotten. We will see our little boy with the sweet little voice again. I can almost hear him say, "I love you, Mamaw. I will reply, "I love you, Austin."

The loss of a child is noted to be the worst pain anyone can experience. I could relate to Jack and Renee and their pain of losing their firstborn son, Austin. I lost my son, Michael W. Lee, my firstborn son (Renee Haley's uncle) because of a fatal car wreck when he was only twenty-one years old.

God is the answer to any trial we face. "The Lord is close to the brokenhearted and saves those who are crushed in spirit; a righteous man may have many troubles, but the Lord delivers him out of them all" (Psalms 34:18–19). We miss our precious little boy. Heaven is sweeter now.

—Great-grandmother (Mamaw)
Dixie Gillum

# Appendix:
## Comforting Bible Verses during Grief and Sadness

The Lord also will be a refuge for the oppressed, a refuge in times of trouble.

*Psalm 9:9*

The Lord is my rock and my fortress and my deliverer; my God, my strength, in whom I will trust; my shield and the horn of my salvation, my stronghold.

*Psalm 18:2*

For he has not despised nor abhorred the affliction of the afflicted; nor has He hidden his face from Him; But when He cried to Him, He heard.

*Psalm 22:24*

The Lord is my shepherd; I shall not want. He makes me to lie down in green pastures; he leads me beside the still waters. He restores my soul; He leads me in the paths of righteousness for his name's sake. Yea, though I walk through the valley of the shadow of death, I will fear no evil; for you are with me; Your rod and Your staff, they comfort me. You prepare a table before me in the presence of my enemies; You anoint my head with oil; my cup runs over. Surely goodness and mercy shall follow me all the days of my life; and I will dwell in the house of the Lord forever.

*Psalm 23*

One thing I have desired of the Lord, that will I seek: that I may dwell in the house of the Lord all the days of my life, to behold the beauty of the Lord and to inquire in his temple. For in the day of trouble He shall hide me in His pavilion; in the secret place of His tabernacle he shall hide me; He shall set me high upon a rock.

Psalm 27:4–5

Weeping may endure for a night, but joy comes in the morning.

Psalm 30:5

The Lord is near to those who have a broken heart, and saves such as have a contrite spirit.

Psalm 34:18

The salvation of the righteous is from the Lord; he is their strength in the time of trouble.

Psalm 37:39

God is our refuge and strength, a very present help in trouble. Therefore we will not fear, even though the earth be removed, and though the mountains be carried into the midst of the sea.

Psalm 46:1–2

For this is God, our God for ever and ever; he will be our guide even to death.

Psalm 48:14

Cast your burden, on the Lord and he shall sustain you; he shall never permit the righteous to be moved.

Psalm 55:22

You who have shown me severe and great troubles, shall revive me again, and bring me up again from the depths of the earth. You shall increase my greatness, and comfort me on every side.

Psalm 71:20–21

My flesh and my heart may fail, but God is the strength of my heart and my portion forever.

Psalm 73:26

Though I walk in the midst of trouble, you will revive me; you will stretch out your hand against the wrath of my enemies, and your right hand will save me.
Psalm 138:7

The wicked is banished in his wickedness, but the righteous has a refuge in his death.
Proverbs 14:32

He will swallow up death forever, and the Lord God will wipe away tears from all faces; the rebuke of His people He will take away from all the earth; for the Lord has spoken.
Isaiah 25:8

Have you not known? Have you not heard? The everlasting God, the Lord, the creator of the ends of the earth, neither faints nor is weary. His understanding is unsearchable. He gives power to the weak, and to those who have no might He increases strength. Even the youths shall faint and be weary, and the young men shall utterly fall, but those who wait on the Lord shall renew their strength; they shall mount up with wings like eagles, they shall run and not be weary, they shall walk and not faint.
Isaiah 40:28–31

But Zion said, "The Lord has forsaken me, and my Lord has forgotten me." Can a woman forget her nursing child, and not have compassion on the son of her womb? Surely they may forget, yet I will not forget you. See, I have inscribed you on the palms of My hands; your walls are continually before Me.
Isaiah 49:14–16

For the Lord will comfort Zion, He will comfort all her waste places; he will make her wilderness like Eden, and her desert like the garden of the Lord; joy and gladness will be found in it, thanksgiving and the voice of melody.
Isaiah 51:3

For the mountains shall depart and the hills be removed, but my kindness shall not depart from you, nor shall my covenant of peace be removed, says the Lord, who has mercy on you.
Isaiah 54:10

For thus says the Lord: Behold, I will extend peace to her like a river, and the glory of the Gentiles like a flowing stream. Then you shall feed; on her sides shall you be carried, and be dandled on her knees. As one whom his mother comforts, so I will comfort you; and you shall be comforted in Jerusalem.
Isaiah 66:12–14

For the Lord will not cast off forever. Though He causes grief, yet he will show compassion according to the multitude of His mercies. For He does not afflict willingly, nor grieve the children of men.
Lamentations 3:31–33

I will ransom them from the power of the grave; I will redeem them from death. O Death, I will be your plagues! O Grave, I will be your destruction! Pity is hidden from My eyes.
Hosea 13:14

The LORD is good, a stronghold in the day of trouble; and He knows those who trust in Him.
Nahum 1:7

Blessed are those who mourn, for they shall be comforted.
Matthew 5:4

Do not lay up for yourselves treasures on earth, where moth and rust destroy and where thieves break in and steal; but lay up for yourselves treasures in heaven, where neither moth nor rust destroys and where thieves do not break in and steal. For where your treasure is, there your heart will be also.
Matthew 6:19–21

Come to Me, all you who labor and are heavy laden, and I will give you rest. Take My yoke upon you and learn from Me, for I am gentle and lowly in heart, and you will find rest for your souls. For My yoke is easy and My burden is light.
Matthew 11:28–30

This is the will of the Father who sent Me, that of all He has given Me I should lose nothing, but should raise it up at the last day. And this is the will of Him who sent Me, that everyone who sees the Son and believes in Him may have everlasting life; and I will raise him up at the last day.

John 6:39–40

Let not your heart be troubled; you believe in God, believe also in Me. In My Father's house are many mansions; if it were not so, I would have told you. I go to prepare a place for you, and if I go and prepare a place for you, I will come again and receive you to Myself; that where I am, there you may be also. And where I go you know, and the way you know.

John 14:1–4

Peace I leave with you; my peace I give to you; not as the world gives do I give to you. Let not your heart be troubled, neither let it be afraid.

John 14:27

For as many as are led by the Spirit of God, these are sons of God. For you did not receive the spirit of bondage again to fear, but you received the Spirit of adoption by whom we cry out, "Abba, Father."

Romans 8:14–15

What then shall we say to these things? If God is for us, who can be against us? He who did not spare His own Son, but delivered Him up for us all, how shall He not with Him also freely give us all things? Who shall bring a charge against God's elect? It is God who justifies. Who is he who condemns? It is Christ who died, and furthermore is also risen, who is even at the right hand of God, who also makes intercession with us. Who shall separate us from the love of Christ? Shall tribulation, or distress, or persecution, or famine, or nakedness, or peril, or sword? As it is written: For Your sake we are killed all day long; we are accounted as sheep for the slaughter. Yet in all of those things we are more than conquerors though Him who loved us. For I am persuaded that neither death nor life, nor angels nor principalities nor powers, nor things present nor things to come, nor height nor depth, nor any other created thing, shall be able to separate us from the love of God which is in Christ Jesus our Lord.

Romans 8:31–39

In a moment, in the twinkling of an eye, at the last trumpet. For the trumpet will sound, and the dead will be raised incorruptible, and we shall be changed. For this corruptible must put on incorruption, and this mortal must put on immortality. So when this corruptible has put on incorruption, and this mortal has put on immortality, then shall be brought to pass the saying that is written: "Death is swallowed up in victory." O Death, where is your sting? O Hades, where is your victory? The sting of death is sin, and the strength of sin is the law. But thanks be to God, who gives us the victory through our Lord Jesus Christ.

1 Corinthians 15:52–57

Blessed be the God and Father of our Lord Jesus Christ, the Father of mercies and God of all comfort, who comforts us in all our tribulation, that we may be able to comfort those who are in any trouble, with the comfort with which we ourselves are comforted by God. For as the sufferings of Christ abound in us, so our consolation also abounds through Christ.

2 Corinthians 1:3–5

According to what is written, "I believed and therefore I spoke," we also believe and therefore speak, knowing that He who raised up the Lord Jesus will also raise us up with Jesus, and will present us with you. For all things are for your sakes, that grace, having spread through the many, may cause thanksgiving to abound to the glory of God. Therefore we do not lose heart. Even though our outward man is perishing, yet the inward man is being renewed day by day.

2 Corinthians 4:13–16

And he said to me, "My grace is sufficient for you, for my strength is made perfect in weakness." Therefore most gladly I will rather boast in my infirmities, that the power of Christ may rest upon me. Therefore I take pleasure in infirmities, in reproaches, in needs, in persecutions, in distresses, for Christ's sake. For when I am weak, then I am strong.

2 Corinthians 12:9–10

Be anxious for nothing, but in everything by prayer and supplication, with thanksgiving, let your requests be made known to God.

Philippians 4:6

## Appendix

But I do not want you to be ignorant, brethren, concerning those who have fallen asleep, lest you sorrow as others who have no hope.

I Thessalonians 4:13

Since the children have flesh and blood, he too shared in their humanity so that by his death he might destroy him who holds the power of death—that is, the devil—and free those who all their lives were held in slavery by their fear of death.

Hebrews 2:14–15

Inasmuch then as the children have partaken of flesh and blood, He Himself likewise shared in the same, that through death He might destroy him who had the power of death, that is, the devil, and release those who through fear of death were all their lifetime subject to bondage. For indeed He does not give aid to angels, but He does give aid to the seed of Abraham.

Hebrews 4:14–16

Blessed be the God and Father of our Lord Jesus Christ, who according to His abundant mercy has begotten us again to a living hope through the resurrection of Jesus Christ from the dead, to an inheritance incorruptible and undefiled and that does not fade away, reserved in heaven for you, who are kept by the power of God through faith for salvation ready to be revealed in the last time. In this you greatly rejoice, though now for a little while, if need be, you have been grieved by various trials, that the genuineness of your faith, being much more precious than gold that perishes, though it is tested by fire, may be found to praise, honor, and glory at the revelation of Jesus Christ, whom having not seen you love. Though now you do not see Him, yet believing, you rejoice with joy inexpressible and full of glory, receiving the end of your faith the salvation of your souls.

I Peter 1:3–9

Therefore, humble yourselves under the mighty hand of God, that he may exalt you in due time, casting all your care upon Him, for He cares for you.

I Peter 5:6–7

These are the ones who come out of the great tribulation, and washed their robes and made them white in the blood of the Lamb. Therefore they are before the throne of God, and serve Him day and night in His temple. And he who sits on the throne will dwell among them. They shall neither hunger anymore nor thirst anymore; the sun shall not strike them, nor any heat; for the Lamb who is in the midst of the throne will shepherd them and lead them to living fountains of waters. And God will wipe every tear from their eyes.
Revelation 7:14–17

And God will wipe away every tear from their eyes; there shall be no more death, nor sorrow, nor crying. There shall be no more pain, for the former things have passed away.
Revelation 21:4

# Unforgettable Quotes from Family and Friends

Dalton (brother) when waking up on Austin's birthday: "Mama, today is Austin's birthday, and they are having a big party for him in heaven; I want to go—I promise I will come back."

Dalton to Grandma Cheryl: "Grandma, I have a puzzle of all the states that I put together. Would you show me where heaven is on my puzzle?"

Cheryl (grandma): "Austin went from the joy of fishing with his grandpa into the arms of Jesus."

Cheryl: "I can't put my finger on it, but this child is very, very special because of all the things Austin has said regarding his deep love for God at such a young age."

Cheryl: "Our grandbaby. Why? Why? Why?" (falling to her knees)

Bettie (grandma): "It's murder in my opinion."

Bettie: (grandma): "I miss the hugs and kisses I would get from Austin. He was such a special little boy."

Dixie (great-grandma): "Austin, baby, you never cease to amaze me—the beautiful things you say about Jesus."

Dixie: "Austin, God's got His hand on you, sweetheart. God is really going to use you one day."

Michelle (aunt): Intercessory Prayer: "God, place the heavy burden on me that my sister is carrying so she can make it through this extremely difficult time of losing her son. Allow me to help carry the load." (Michelle was extremely heavily burdened for a long time).

Sandy (aunt): I had the opportunity to babysit Austin for a couple of years. We would often sing the song from Petra called "We Need Jesus" together in the car. I still remember his little voice singing along: "And we shall live forever … when we share the love of Jesus." We spent many times watching his favorite television shows: *Sesame Street, Dora the Explorer,* and *Bob the Builder.* I'm better for having known him—we all are.

Barbara (aunt): "He would always run through the door and give me a smile of recognition when he was coming to my shop to get his hair trimmed."

Travis (uncle): "God, I know You were dealing with me about some things and You were trying to get my attention, but, God, not this!"

Justin (cousin): "God is going to use Austin's situation to touch people's lives all over the world."

Baylie (cousin): "Austin is in heaven, and he is *so* happy" (three years old).

Colin Deaton (friend): "Austin was really nice, and I remember playing T-ball with him" (age seven).

Jackson Pensoneau (friend): "Austin was my very best friend. We really liked to play with each other. We really had a good time together. Austin got shot, and he died. I feel really, really sad about it. Austin is happy in heaven. He's eating a really big ice cream sundae" (age seven).

Seth Tennison (friend): "Austin was my best friend. I miss him very much" (age seven).

Noah Standridge (friend): "Austin was a really good friend. I liked to play blocks with him. Austin was kind and honest" (age seven).

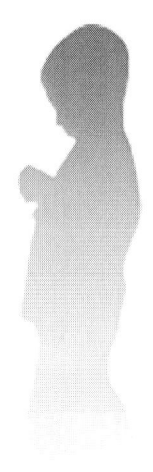

# Endnotes

1 "Children's Understanding of Death." Child Bereavement Charity. 2009. 2 June 2009 <http://www.childbereavement.org.uk/for_schools/children_s_understanding_of_death>
2 "The Compassionate Friends, Inc." 2009. 3 June 2009 http://www.compassionatefriends.org/Media/Surveys.aspx